POLICY AND PRACTICE IN HEALTH AND SOCIAL CARE
NUMBER NINETEEN

Self-directed Support

POLICY AND PRACTICE IN HEALTH AND SOCIAL CARE

See www.dunedinacademicpress.co.uk for details of all our publications

POLICY AND PRACTICE IN HEALTH AND SOCIAL CARE

SERIES EDITORS

ALISON PETCH and CHARLOTTE PEARSON

Self-directed Support: Personalisation, Choice and Control

Charlotte Pearson

Lecturer in Social & Public Policy,
Institute of Health & Well-Being,
University of Glasgow

Julie Ridley

Reader in Applied Social Science,
University of Central Lancashire

and

Susan Hunter

Honorary Fellow, School of Social and Political Science,
University of Edinburgh

EDINBURGH ◆ LONDON

First published in 2014 by Dunedin Academic Press Ltd.
Head Office: Hudson House, 8 Albany Street, Edinburgh EH1 3QB
London Office: 352 Cromwell Tower, Barbican, London EC2Y 8NB

ISBNs:
978-1-78046-024-6 (Paperback)
978-1-78046-522-7 (ePub)
978-1-78046-523-4 (Kindle)

ISSN: 1750-1407

British Library Cataloguing in Publication data
A catalogue record for this book is available at the British Library

Typeset by Makar Publishing Production
Printed in Great Britain by CPI Antony Rowe

CONTENTS

SERIES EDITORS' INTRODUCTION

Some time ago, Charlotte Pearson produced the second volume in this series. With 'Personalisation' in the title, that book has attracted renewed interest in recent years as the term became increasingly familiar as a shorthand for a person-centred approach, an emphasis on the individual and on choice. We approached the author and asked if she would like to prepare an updated edition. She responded with a more exciting suggestion – a new volume that would focus on self-directed support (SDS) and would draw in addition on the expertise of two co-authors. Although SDS is just one element of a wider personalisation agenda, the prospective implementation of new legislation in Scotland from April 2014 made this a particularly attractive proposition.

Chapter 1 reminds us of the history of cash-for-care schemes and the leading role of the disability movement in their promotion. It also sets out an important distinction between direct payments and personal budgets. Chapter 2 explores the changing policy directives in social welfare and the emergence of co-production as a key driver both in Scotland and farther afield. It introduces the critical dimensions of social justice, equity and risk. Chapter 3 offers insights into practical implementation from the three SDS test sites in Scotland, drawing on evaluation led by one of the authors. Challenges associated with self-assessment and with resource allocation systems are highlighted. Chapter 4 provides a very interesting reflection on the potential impact of SDS on professional roles; if SDS achieves its full potential, the role of professional support is likely to be very different. The final chapter considers the extent to which the aspirations for choice and control inherent in a more personalised delivery can be achieved in a period of austerity or whether they are inevitably compromised.

A key strength of this volume is that it gets beyond the immediate concerns of SDS implementation, the 'who, what, when', and the specifics of the four options that are preoccupying the workforce in the immediate aftermath of the legislation. It reminds us of the broader principles that underlie the concept and the aspirations of those who first argued for the approach. It offers an important benchmark for ongoing critical appraisal of both the policy and the practice of SDS in particular and personalisation more broadly.

It is a particular pleasure that publication of this book marks Charlotte Pearson's new role as a series editor for Policy and Practice in Health and Social Care, in succession to Joyce Cavaye, whose sterling work as a founding editor has helped establish the series' place in the literature scrutinising the health and social care issues of a modern democratic state and the Scottish response to the challenges faced

Professor Alison Petch
The Institute for Research and Innovation in Social Services (IRISS), Glasgow

LIST OF ABBREVIATIONS

ADASS	Association of Directors of Adult Social Services
ADSW	Association of Directors of Social Work
ASPA	Adult Support and Protection Act 20007
CIL	Centres for Independent/Inclusive Living
COSLA	Convention of Scottish Local Authorities
CRPD	Convention on the Rights of Persons with Disabilities
DLA	Disability Living Allowance
DP	Direct payment
DPAC	Disabled People Against the Cuts
ENIL	European Network on Independent Living
IB	Individual Budget
IBSEN	Individual Budgets Evaluation Network
ILF	Independent Living Fund
ILT	Independent Living Transfer
IRISS	Innovation in Social Services
NPG	New Public Governance
NPM	New Public Management
PA	Personal assistant
PB	Personal budget
PIP	Personal Independence Payment
RAS	Resource allocation system
SDS	Self-directed Support
SDSS	Self-directed Support Scotland
SNP	Scottish Nationalist Party
SPAEN	Scottish Personal Assistants Employers Network

CHAPTER 1

Introduction

Over the past thirty years, there has been a gradual shift in social care provision towards an increasingly personalised framework of support, whereby individual users are more involved in the choice of services they are assessed as needing. They can have the option of purchasing these through a cash payment, which is paid directly to them (Arksey and Kemp, 2008). With new legislation for self-directed support (SDS) implemented in Scotland in April 2014, social care has entered a new era, heralding a major cultural shift for both users and service professionals. By drawing on a range of literature and empirical findings that have underpinned the emergence of policies in Scotland, the UK and across Europe, this book sets out to unravel some of the key debates. In doing this, it will set out the framework to explore the conceptual changes, the renegotiation of professional roles and the impact on users, particularly as legislation emerges at a time of economic downturn.

Before setting out these ideas in more detail, however, it is important to recognise the origins of policy development and establish the backdrop of disability activism, which initiated these changes. We therefore begin by outlining how a campaign by a small number of disabled people informed a long-term global shift in the reorganisation and delivery of social care services. Discussion then moves to explore how direct payments (DP) policy emerged on the statute and yet led to only marginal use across the UK, especially in Scotland. Despite acknowledging the importance of an increasingly individualised model of social care, the implementation of DP policy has waned in the past decade, and successive central and local governments – north and south of the border – have embraced a new focus on 'personalisation'. In looking at some of the broader themes through which policy emerged, this chapter concludes by detailing an outline of the book and a summary of the terms that will be used.

The campaign for personalised support: The role of disability activism

The idea of cash-for-care-based support schemes as an alternative to directly organised services originated in the 1970s in the US (Arksey and Kemp, 2008). At this time, a small group of students with physical impairments at the University of Berkeley secured the payment of cash in place of services to buy in support that fitted with their daily needs on campus. Gradually, news of this spread throughout the US, and by the 1980s similar challenges were being made by groups of disabled people in the UK (Campbell and Oliver, 1996).

As described in Pearson (2006), throughout the 1980s and 1990s indirect payments – those administered through third parties such as voluntary sector organisations or independent local trusts – were used to overcome legal restrictions to a cash-based model of support across the UK. Prior to this time, the 1948 Social Security Act covering England and Wales had stipulated that only services – not payments – could be made by local authorities, while the position differed slightly in Scotland. Provisions set out in Section 12 of the 1968 Social Work (Scotland) Act allowed cash payments to be made available by local authorities in exceptional circumstances (Roll, 1996). However, the impact of this ruling was limited, as there was only minimal knowledge of this guidance among local authority practitioners (Pearson, 2000), and evidence of only one area making payments through this route (Witcher et al., 2000).

In line with actions a few years earlier in the US, the roles of small groups of disabled people were central to changes during the 1980s and 1990s. They demanded a more flexible alternative to rigid and paternalistic modes of service provision offered to them by local authorities. Most of this activism occurred in England, where disabled people in areas such as Hampshire, Essex, Norfolk and Derbyshire initiated these challenges. In Scotland, although developments were more limited, pockets of activism also emerged during the 1980s, notably in the former Lothian region. At this time, Lothian Regional Council permitted three indirect payments to be made. While this was initially approved, problems arose when, in 1995, the then Department of Social Security was alerted to this practice and suspended all the Income Support payments of those involved. This resulted from a circular issued by the Department of Health, which stated that all forms of DP made through local authorities were illegal. Consequently, a challenge to the case in Lothian was made and won by the local authority, but the case had raised the profile and potential of cash payments to increase disabled people's choice and control over their social care, thereby instigating the need for a formal legislative path to be developed (Pearson, 2004).

Other examples of indirect payments in Scotland pre-1996 also emerged at this time in light of wider policy shifts from central government (see Pearson, 2006). In the former Strathclyde region, monies paid from the Independent Living Transfer (ILT) helped establish an alternative model of indirect payments. These were made available to local authorities as community care was being rolled out, to allow them to develop 'independent living' services for disabled people in the area. Unlike the payments being made in response to the demands of disabled people in key local authorities, funding for this approach came from central government. This emerged from wider changes amid a reorganisation of social security for disabled people and the development of community care policy from the late 1980s (Glendinning, 1992) by the then Conservative government. Part of this strategy also included the launch of the Independent Living Fund (ILF), which allowed another route to indirect payments to emerge for a key group of disabled people (see Kestenbaum, 1992). Importantly, the availability of these payments through the ILF – a charity funded by central government – enabled an additional stream of cash payments to support independent living to be made available to those with the highest support needs and replace residential care as the only alternative. Since this time, the ILF has played an important role in the genesis of personalised support, facilitating increased choice and flexibility in the lives of its recipients (Morris, 2004). It has been widely popular with users, and as Jane Campbell points out: 'The ILF has enabled people such as me to learn, work, volunteer, play and live in a way that has met our needs and allowed us to be active members of the society we live in' (Campbell, 2014). As discussion in Chapter

5 sets out, its proposed closure in parts of the UK in 2015 therefore signifies a major setback to the independent living choices to a key cohort of disabled people across the country.

Although some local authorities were developing indirect payment schemes for small groups of users, disability activists across the UK were keen to secure a legal statute so that cash-based provision could be secured for all those who would like it. Legislation for DPs was eventually implemented in England and Wales, with the Community Care (Direct Payments) Act 1995, and in Scotland through the Scotland Act 1996. An initially reluctant Conservative government was finally persuaded to adopt the Acts after publication of research into personal assistance schemes by the British Council of Disabled People (see Zarb and Nadash, 1994) showed DPs to be around 40% cheaper than directly provided services. This proved to be an attractive pull for an administration committed to an agenda of cost-savings and efficiency. The policy framework for DPs therefore developed through both independent living and market discourses (Pearson, 2000). On the one hand, campaigning from the disability movement at both national and local levels was important in establishing momentum for change. However, on the other hand as noted, the appeal for the Conservative government rested in its positioning of DPs as part of a wider marketisation of care established through the 1990 Community Care Act. This framed DPs – and subsequently personalisation – as an instrument for facilitating choice and diversity in service provision while increasing cost-effectiveness through the development of local care markets.

DPs and personal budgets (PBs) have often been confused as being essentially the same thing – in that they both involve a cash alternative to directly provided services. However, as Beresford (2009) notes, there are important differences in their underpinning ideologies. As set out above, DPs were a grassroots development emerging from the disabled people's movement and a desire to equalise opportunities and increase independent living, while PBs evolved from developments largely driven by professionals critical of the welfare state and its ability to promote independent living. DPs are based on a social model of disability and the philosophy of independent living, whereas 'personalisation' evolved from the vision of welfare reformers such as those responsible for *In Control* – pioneers of SDS and Individual Budgets (IBs) in 2003 as an approach to enable disabled people to direct and take charge of their support – which has since influenced national policy promoting personalisation. Although inspired by the independent living movement, the motivation for personalisation comes from a desire to reform an outmoded social care system, influenced by a model developed by *In Control* alongside people with learning difficulties. Its associated with the philosophy of 'normalisation', which is typically concerned with integrating disabled people into society, rather than challenging its barriers and discrimination. It was also intended that DPs would be set at a level that would enable independent living. By contrast, personalisation has been set on a basis of available funding through the controversial 'resource allocation system' (RAS) (see chapters 3 and 5 for more detailed consideration of implementation of the RAS). As detailed in the next section, its emergence on the national policy stage also reflects a starkly different path.

The rise and fall of direct payments and the rise and rise of personalisation

While the emergence of DP legislation was undoubtedly seen as a victory for the independent living movement (Pearson, 2000), its implementation was characterised by inconsistent take-up across the UK (Riddell *et al.*, 2005), with the number of users in Scotland, Wales and Northern Ireland especially low when compared with key local authorities in the south of England such as Hampshire and Essex. From 1997 to 2003, various attempts were made by the (then) Scottish Executive and Westminster governments to reignite policy, but uptake was never more than marginal (Priestley *et al.*, 2010; Pearson, 2004). From the outset, implementation was not mandatory, leaving potential users reliant on social workers to act as 'gate keepers' to a DP (Ellis, 2007). Revised legislation north and south of the border in 2002 placed a mandatory duty on all local authorities to offer DPs, but the pace of uptake remained slow, over-bureaucratic and limited by funding constraints. By contrast, the political will to implement personalisation assumed a much faster pace (Riddell *et al.*, 2005).

Under the Labour Government (1997–2010) many of the themes that linked DPs to the Conservatives' broader agenda of marketisation were developed through a focus on the personalisation of social care services. At this stage, ideas promoted by Leadbeater (2004; 2008) – exploring how services could be modernised through the direct participation of users in service delivery – had a profound influence on reforming the adult social care system. Leadbeater (2008, p. 47) argued strongly in favour of the model of consumerism that envisaged users taking on the role of a budget holder, but they also emphasised its link with citizenship with its related rights and entitlements. However, as Carr (2013) and others (Rummery, 2006; Morris, 2004) state, his approach to citizenship did not necessarily fit with individual identities and the experiences of people who use social care and mental health services.

The Labour Government also oversaw the publication of the cross-departmental strategy to transform the structure of services for disabled people; it was entitled *Improving the Life Chances of Disabled People* (Cabinet Office, 2005). As detailed elsewhere (see Pearson, 2006), it was widely welcomed by disabled people's organisations for its wide-ranging focus on independent living and the need to engage in reform across key policy areas such as health, housing, social care, education and transport to achieve this. One of the key messages highlighted in *Improving the Life Chances of Disabled People* was the need to promote disabled people's expertise in developing support structures, rather than relying on professional control. Drawing on the experiences of DP, PB and ILF users, *Improving the Life Chances of Disabled People* also demonstrated the need for a more flexible system of social care where some disabled people wanted more control of resources, while others were daunted by taking a DP and organising their own support.

As Beresford (2009, p. 1) observes, from this time what was set out as little more than a vague idea in the mid-2000s seemed to become 'an unstoppable force' over the next ten years. Personalisation in social care has undoubtedly represented a major shift in public policy. Beresford (2013) and others (see Boxall *et al.*, 2009) highlight its ascendancy in England, with the allocation of a relatively large amount of funding in social care – £500 million – to take it forward.

In Scotland, the shift to a more personalised system of social care has been slower and – as Kettle *et al.* (2011) note – complex, perhaps reflecting a less enthusiastic drive towards the marketisation of social care in Scotland than south of the border. Hence as policy emerged, the Scottish Government employed the term SDS to develop distinctive policy goals (Manthorpe *et al.*, 2014), setting out SDS to be part of its aspirations to create a 'healthier nation with stronger and safer communities' (Scottish Government, 2007, p. 2).

The subsequent introduction of legislation for SDS was developed through the Social Care (Self-directed Support) (Scotland) Act 2013 (Scottish Government, 2013) and offered four different options for SDS – ranging from a DP approach to support arranged through the local authority (these are set out in chapters 2 and 3). This sought to consolidate the existing – and often complex – provision. Unlike previous administrations, the ruling Scottish National Party's (SNP) support for this legislative path focused on bringing SDS into the mainstream of social care provision and thereby increasing the numbers of people directing their own support from the time of implementation of the Act in April 2014. While the Scottish Government has been enthusiastic in their support for SDS, the main drive for policy implementation has come from the Association of Directors of Social Work (ADSW; now Social Work Scotland) (Kettle *et al.*, 2011). Unlike in England, where the Department of Health has been directive in the rolling out of personalisation including setting targets for the implementation of PBs, the Scottish Government has worked with the Convention of Scottish Local Authorities (COSLA) to encourage local authorities and their partners to progress with SDS in a way that is most suitable for local conditions (Scottish Government, 2010).

Progression in Scotland towards personalisation has been directly linked to ideas set out in the policy document *Changing Lives: Report of the 21st Century Social Work Review in Scotland* (Scottish Executive, 2006). The review – commissioned under the Labour Government at Holyrood and subsequently developed under successive SNP administrations – draws strongly on Leadbeater's ideas (see Leadbeater and Lownsbrough, 2005) and places personalisation at the core of its strategy. This is located at three levels. Firstly, as a means of *prevention,* designed to build an individual's capacity to manage their own lives. Secondly, personalisation for complex cases enables people to *participate* in shaping and delivering their service solutions. Thirdly, personalisation is framed as a means of *consumer choice*. This links in with broader consumerist discourse, which promotes increased efficiency and reliability in service provision.

Like developments in England, policy implementation has been supported by an additional injection of funds through the SDS Transformation Investment. This has covered funding under four broad themes: local authorities; user information and support projects; provider capacity building activity/projects; and workforce change. Available figures show that the monies allocated to local authorities amounted to around £25 million for the period 2011–15 (personal communication). As we discuss in Chapter 3, plans to roll out SDS in Scotland were also aided by the development of three test-site local authorities, where each of the designated areas trialled systems to promote this new culture of social care supported by Scottish Government grant.

Clearly, both administrations north and south of the border have been committed to the promotion of their respective personalisation projects, and both have ensured the availability of additional funds for the development of these policy drives, even at a time where the broader pattern of spending for social care provision has been severely cut. Overall, the scale of the shift towards a personalised system of social care across the UK is unprecedented internationally (Boxall *et al.*, 2009), and as yet we have limited understanding of how the rolling out of SDS will impact on individual social care users.

Indeed, while proponents such as Leadbeater (2008; 2004) draw strongly on personal narratives in articulating his support for policy, unlike DPs the move to implement the policy of personalisation has not been based in a strong evidence base (Beresford, 2013). Furthermore, as stated earlier in this chapter, whereas DPs were rooted in the independent living movement, personalisation is not a user-led development. The organisations most closely associated with its development – *In Control* , Mencap, the Department of Health Care Services Improvement Partnership and particular local authorities – were either conventional voluntary/third sector or state-related organisations with histories in state and charitable organisations and in managerial and professional roles. For Beresford (2013) and others (Roulstone and Morgan, 2009; Ferguson, 2007), the shift from the original DPs to personalisation reflects a move from a means of empowerment to an underfunded market-based voucher system. Similarly, Zarb (2013) argues that the direct link with independent living has been broken through personalisation and lies largely forgotten. In these terms, Zarb (2013) brands personalisation as 'independent living lite', arguing that it lacks any broader progressive political strategy, but that it is also the result of a disconnect between disabled people's organisations and other user groups.

However, like DPs, a postcode lottery remains a prominent feature of how personalisation has been implemented across the UK. As Beresford (2013) and others (West, 2013; Ridley *et al.*, 2011) observe, some local authorities have used personalisation and/or SDS as little more than a rebranding of existing and traditional arrangements. Others have provided the opportunity to widen access to DPs to a more diverse range of users, while in some cases the move has meant the loss of access to traditional collective services (Needham, 2013; Hall, 2011; Ferguson, 2007), with users having to take on all the responsibilities and risks of running a PB without adequate information or support. There are also examples of more positive experiences, often where a user-led organisation is involved and support is framed much more in line with the principles set out by the disability movement. However, this has tended to focus on the DP element of PBs in England, whereby users are given more freedom in their choice and control over service provision (Slasberg *et al.*, 2012). For Roulstone *et al.* (2013), the current drive towards personalisation represents a halfway position. He argues that there have been genuine attempts to listen to organisations of disabled people and that personalisation is clearly counter to a paternalistic system of social care, which delivers services according to professional rather than users' assessment of needs. Yet the term and its use risk dilution, as limited funding and the focus on social care priorities centre on residualised provision, rather than being based on a broader strategy to facilitate independent living.

Outline of the book

Over the next five chapters, we will explore many of these issues in more detail. This begins in Chapter 2, where the framework of definitions and conceptual changes that have emerged through the development of SDS are set out. Central to this shift has been a realignment of the ideas and cultural environment in which the legislation emerges. This includes a focus on the visions and values for policy change and a critical appraisal of the principles of co-production which have been strongly promoted throughout this process. As discussion will show, co-production has been utilised as the basis to involve users with their care managers and service providers to determine their support packages. Inevitably, this raises broader questions around issues of equity and social justice.

Chapter 3 considers what can be learnt from pilots where ideas to transform social care radically have been applied, by looking at some of the early evidence of policy implementation through an evaluation of three SDS test sites funded by the Scottish Government and run between 2009 and 2011. Drawing on the experience of the three test sites, alongside that of other local authorities across the UK implementing IBs and SDS, the chapter considers the evolving concept of SDS and how it relates to DP systems, as well as the challenges for local authorities arising from introducing 'upfront' budget allocations, systems of supported self-assessment, and panels to make decisions about resource allocation.

Chapter 4 explores the impact of SDS implementation on the various supporting roles. By drawing on test site findings from a survey of front-line staff, reflections from voluntary sector providers and studies examining the personal assistant (PA) workforce, discussion focuses on the implications for training and development of social workers and care managers. The chapter reflects on the implications for support roles as SDS becomes increasingly formalised in Scotland, and the extent to which personalisation and SDS are transforming social care. It also examines the extent of user involvement in the strategic development of SDS in Scotland.

Commentary in Chapter 5 looks in more detail at the implications for developing more personalised models of social care in an era of acute economic austerity. As the financial crisis of 2008 took hold, we examine the impact of this both in Scotland and across Europe as governments have sought to realign their spending priorities. For many, the focus of choice and control at the heart of the personalisation agenda has been dramatically compromised as the socio-economic position of disabled people has been eroded through a series of austerity cuts. We examine here how governments have reacted to economic conditions. In many cases, this has led to direct cuts to support for disabled people and a major erosion of the principles of independent living. In other examples, we show how governments have been forced to change tack and make compromises in some of the more draconian aspects of their welfare reform programme.

Chapter 6 concludes by reviewing the book themes. We highlight the main debates and issues emanating from earlier chapters and set out a focus on innovative practice and the use of co-production techniques in small local projects around the UK. In recognition of the acute austerity impacting on social care spending, we review some of the wider critical commentary in this area and explore an agenda for moving forward with personalisation.

Use of terminology in the book

It is clear from the history of DPs, personalisation, SDS and other cash-for-care based schemes in social care that the terms can be used interchangeably and are confusing. As Beresford (2013) points out, 'personalisation' as a term has no clear or agreed meaning. He argues that, while originally it was used to describe people accessing a cash budget (PB or IB) to spend on their support and put together what help and services they wanted, more recently there has been a shift in the term's official usage. It is now used more generically by the Westminster government to mean people having more choice and control and a more customised service, regardless of what service or form of support they receive, and however it is provided. Given the shift to a more generic definition of personalisation, throughout this book we will use it as an umbrella term to encapsulate the range of different approaches both in the UK and farther afield. Where we focus specifically on policy developments in Scotland, we will refer to the appropriate aspect of the SDS legislation. Likewise the English system of PBs will also be differentiated where appropriate.

The terms IB and PB are frequently used interchangeably but have been adopted to mean different things (Leece and Leece, 2011). IBs were intended to bring money together from different funding streams such as Supporting People, Access to Work, health and local authority funding, though in practice this has rarely happened (Rosengard *et al.*, 2013; Ridley *et al.*, 2011; Glendinning *et al.*, 2008). PBs meanwhile were to refer to local authorities' community care funding. Prior to implementation of SDS legislation in Scotland, some local authorities used IBs as a means to promote more flexible support arrangements. They allowed a person to know how much money was available for their support, thereby giving them maximum choice over how the funds were spent. This could mean that they took the full IB as a DP, or it could involve more complex approaches where, for example, a social worker or appointed third party manages the full amount on the individual's behalf. So money might not actually change hands, but critically the individual knew how much was available to be spent on their own needs and chose how this was organised. In Scotland – as we set out in Chapter 2 – the shift to SDS has also incorporated different approaches based on how individual resources are managed. These have been organised into four options, only one of which offers the user a DP model of a cash payment. It is therefore clear that SDS has assumed a number of definitions and, as we outline in Chapter 3, remains an evolving concept.

A system of personalised support referred to in this book is the SDS model pioneered and promoted by *In Control* in 2003, which was developed through work with people with learning difficulties and their families. The *In Control* model utilised a seven-step plan for users working with their supporters to identify their needs, and it includes targets to plan how the money is spent as well as support organised in line with user wishes. The *In Control* SDS model involves local councils identifying an 'upfront' or indicative IB, and developing a RAS through which it is decided how much money is available to them to fund their support arrangements (Rabiee *et al.*, 2009). As discussion in Chapter 3 shows, the *In Control* approach has been influential in many local authority responses to SDS.

Conclusions

This chapter has set out the background to debates around person-alisation in social care in Scotland and England. In doing this, we have shown how the role of disability activism formed the major impetus for policy implementation in DPs in the late 1990s. As DPs failed to secure a mainstream role in social care provision, discussion moved to outline how successive Labour and Coalition governments at Westminster embraced a focus on personalisation and promoted it as part of their broader plans for welfare reform. By 2006, *Changing Lives: Report of the 21st Century Social Work Review in Scotland* (Scottish Executive, 2006) put forward an agenda for change, establishing personalisation as the basis to pursue this. As detailed, this formed the basis of the legislative path for SDS policy in Scotland.

CHAPTER 2

Changing Definitions and Values in New Cultures of Care

Introduction

This chapter sets out the underlying visions and values of SDS. In exploring these debates, we examine one of the central themes of the new SDS legislation in Scotland in more detail – the notion of co-production. Discussion shows how the term has evolved amid the wider competing discourses of managerialism and consumerism, which have infiltrated social care policy over the past twenty years. The chapter shows that rather than displace these ideas, co-production now forms an integral part of modernisation programmes for social welfare, including the development of a framework for SDS policy in Scotland (Scottish Government, 2010). This was adopted initially under Labour – both in Westminster and Holyrood – and subsequently taken on by the Coalition and SNP administrations. In this context, we discuss the issues and contradictions around equity and social justice, and the chapter concludes by reviewing debates around risk, advocacy and self-determination.

Self-directed support in an age of personalisation

The adoption of the Convention on the Rights of Persons with Disabilities (CRPD) by the UN Assembly in 2006 marked the culmination of many years of work within the UN system to place disability rights on the international agenda and to integrate disability issues fully into the broader human rights and international development framework (Power *et al.*, 2013). CRPD served as an impetus for disability law and policy reform at both domestic and regional levels and defined a framework from which to understand the concept of personalisation and operationalisation in both law and policy. As Chapter 1 set out, the concept of personalisation reflects a shift away from passive, paternalistic provision of services for disabled people and instead embraces individual decision-making and autonomy, which allows greater choice and self-determination over how needs are met.

Discussion in Chapter 1 outlined the origins of this shift in Scotland through the sporadic appearance of local cash-for-care-based payment schemes in the 1980s and 1990s, until legislation was secured on the statute through the 1996 Community Care (Direct Payments) (Scotland) Act. To recap, revised legislation enacted from April 2003 through the 2002 Community Care and Health (Scotland) Act stipulated that DPs should be made available as a service option to anyone assessed as having community care needs. Although uptake of DPs has varied considerably across the country (Riddell *et al.*, 2005), DPs never gained the mainstream support that many in the disability movement hoped for, and usage in Scotland has remained particularly low (Pearson, 2006; Witcher *et al.*, 2000). By contrast, endorsement of personalisation as a theme for the reform of social care has received unilateral support from all major political parties, and from local and central governments north and south of the border, and it now underpins social care legislation in Scotland with the passing of the 2013 Act.

Chapter 1 also set out how personalisation has become an umbrella term encapsulating a range of different approaches, including DPs, IBs (Glendinning *et al.*, 2008) and SDS (Leadbeater, 2008; Leadbeater, 2004) emphasising choice, control and flexibility in social care support. Slasberg *et al.* (2013) have usefully distinguished between the three components that form the basis of the policy framework in England and Wales. Firstly, they define personalisation as the overarching ambition of the legislation, giving individuals greater control over their lives. Secondly, a PB (or IB) enables the purchase of supports and services most appropriate for the individual. As Manthorpe *et al.* (2011) suggest, this can refer to the design and delivery of public services in accordance with the identified needs and declared requirements of each individual, rather than those of the service commissioner. Thirdly, in England,

SDS can be seen as the process through which the IB is given 'up front' so that the individual can enter the social care market as an 'empowered consumer'. This may be linked to a more political dimension of the personalisation framework, to an intended transformation of relationships between government, service providers and users in social care (Vallelly and Manthorpe, 2009).

Discussion introduced in Chapter 1 showed how, in Scotland with its different legislation and entitlement to flexible support under the Social Care (Self-directed Support) (Scotland) Act 2013, the focus on realigning social care along the lines of personalisation principles has been promoted through a framework for SDS. Throughout its inception, SDS has been described as an 'evolving concept', poorly understood by many practitioners and frequently confused with DPs (Ridley *et al.*, 2011). This is a theme we explore in more detail in Chapter 3, but here we note the somewhat aspirational description of SDS as set out in 2010 *National Strategy*, which viewed SDS as:

> A term that describes the ways in which individuals and families can have informed choice about the way support is provided to them. It includes a range of options for exercising those choices. Through a co-production approach to agreeing individual outcomes, options are considered for ways in which available resources can be used so people can have greater needs over how their support needs are met, and by whom (Scottish Government, 2010, p. 229).

Greater clarity in defining SDS in a Scottish context has emerged through consultation on the SDS Bill and the subsequent passing of the 2013 Act, placing a duty on local authorities to offer users a variety of options. Therefore, unlike Slasberg *et al.'s* (2013) categorisation of SDS in England outlined above, in Scotland the policy for SDS as determined by the 2013 Act incorporated four options:

- The making of a DP by the local authority to the supported person for the provision of support.
- The selection of support by the supported person, the making of arrangements for the provision of it by the local authority on behalf of the supported person and, where it is provided by someone other than the authority, the payment by the local

authority of the relevant amount in respect of the cost of that provision.

- The selection of support for the supported person by the local authority, the making of arrangements for the provision of it by the authority and, where it is provided by someone other than the authority, the payment by the authority of the relevant amount in respect of the cost of that provision.
- The selection by the supported person of Option 1, 2 or 3 for each type of support and, where it is provided by someone other than the authority, the payment by the local authority of the relevant amount in respect of the cost of the support.

In a clear departure from the provisions of the DP legislation, the 2013 Act required local authorities in Scotland to offer the option of support in the form of SDS in the first instance. In doing this, it is stipulated that support should not only reflect users' views but also incorporate self-assessment and be outcome-focused rather than service-focused (Miller, 2012). Earlier initiatives for personalisation in England such as the *In Control* project (see Poll *et al.*, 2006; and Chapter 1, above) were trialled in the Scottish authority of North Lanarkshire (Etherington *et al.*, 2009). This offered a model for policy implementation, particularly through the application of IBs and the use of PAs. While the North Lanarkshire approach set out a clear road map and an appetite for delivery of personalisation in Scotland, the four options set out in the 2013 Act, outlined above, embraced a broader conception of SDS. This has allowed wider options for others to be involved in facilitating and managing the support, and thereby widening SDS from the provision of PAs and self-management of their budget as a DP to having a say over provided services.

Visions and values for SDS

Discussion in the last chapter set out the two conceptual sources from which an agenda for personalisation has emerged: firstly, from sustained activism and campaigning by the disability movement for cash-based support options from which users can control and organise their own support (see Zarb and Nadash, 1994; Kestenbaum, 1992); and, secondly, through the 'new script for public services' set out by Leadbeater (2008; 2004) and Leadbeater and Lownsbrough

(2005), exploring how social and healthcare services could be modernised through the direct participation of users in service delivery. In exploring the policy discourses underpinning these approaches, one has evolved from a strong rights or social justice model (Pearson, 2000), while the other has grown from a more reformist zeal. Ironically, while the disabled people's movement strongly aligned DPs with a rights-based discourse, many working at the front line of policy implementation in Scotland viewed DPs as little more than 'backdoor privatisation' (Pearson, 2004). Various attempts were made by the then Scottish Executive to reinvigorate DPs, culminating in the Health and Social Care Act 2003, which compelled local authorities to offer DPs to all those requesting them. Yet, as shown in Chapter 1, there was never a uniform swing among Scottish local authorities to embrace this model of support.

As policymakers across the UK governments shifted their allegiances from DPs to personalisation within a broader model of welfare reform, it became clear that many of the values underpinning social care in Scotland were going to be subjected to fundamental change. In his 2004 pamphlet, Leadbeater helpfully distinguishes between what he terms 'shallow' personalisation involving 'modest modification' of services, and 'deep personalisation' that engages users as co-designers of services. This has been facilitated through the concept of co-production (Hunter and Ritchie, 2007). Indeed, the principles of co-production have been placed firmly at the heart of the SDS strategy in Scotland, with an emphasis on collective agreement from users and practitioners at all stages of theory and practice development (Scottish Government, 2010). As a central tenet of SDS policy development in Scotland, discourses around co-production are now explored in more detail.

Putting co-production on the social care agenda

As suggested, co-production describes a particular approach to partnership between people who rely on services and the people and agencies providing these services (Hunter and Ritchie, 2007). Policy discussion of SDS has been mostly located in the direct delivery of services to individuals in a manner that increases user satisfaction and improves efficiency by making better use of the resources that both providers and users bring to the table. Over and above the focus on enhanced individual support, classic co-production relates to the generation of social capital – the reciprocal relationships that build trust, peer support and social activism within communities (Needham and Carr, 2009; Loeffler *et al.*, 2008). However, these additional dimensions to co-production, which draw attention to levels of collaboration not only between users and providers but also within neighbourhoods and communities, are acknowledged but have received less attention within the personalisation narrative (Needham, 2011b). This understanding of the potential for co-production to deliver 'added-value' has seeped from professional policy and practice into the conduct of research. In doing this, there has been change in the value of this knowledge to ensure that it is co-produced and users are involved throughout all stages of the process (Verschuere *et al.*, 2012; Armstrong and Alsop, 2010). This shift in mindset from traditional, professional and service-centric relationships to those based on 'equal and reciprocal' (Nesta, 2011) is captured in Table 2.1.

Table 2.1: Co-production and the shifting policy mindset.

From	To
Locus of power with professionals	Locus of power with people who use support
Professional assessment of need	User-defined outcomes
Professional-led mechanisms for service development	New user-led mechanisms for service development
Users as passive recipients	Active participation by people who use services
A 'consumer' in a mixed economy of care	Being an active citizen
A service focus (or even individualised funding)	Capacity-building and embedding within community networks

Source: Cited in Hunter and Rowley (under review).

Furthermore, co-production has recently been described (Ottmann *et al.*, 2011) as re-energised by its conception as synonymous with innovation in public services and by its perceived potential for:

- improving responsiveness and quality of services (Leadbeater and Lownsbrough, 2005);
- increasing effectiveness and reducing costs (Gershon, 2004);

- strengthening citizenship (Vamstad, 2004).

Understanding that co-production is a multi-layered concept, which is helped by taking a brief look at the evolution of this idea. As a broad concept, co-production became familiar in the US with the work of Elinor Ostrom (cited in Ottmann *et al.*, 2011) and has its philosophical roots in the communitarian and collective action ideologies popularised by Arnstein's work on the 'ladder of participation' (1971). By the 1980s and 1990s, it featured centrally within the writings of what became known as the school of New Public Management (NPM) (Pestoff, 2012; Bovaird and Loeffler, 2012). In terms of public service thinking in the UK, Needham and Carr (2009) observe that the focus on co-production in the policy agenda within social care largely disappeared during the 1980s as policymakers favoured such NPM-market approaches to service delivery and an increasingly managerialist culture embedded in social care by the introduction of care management. This emphasised the separate interests of service producers and consumers through the so-called 'purchaser/provider split', rather than the value of collaborative advantage and synergy (Huxham and Vangen, 2005).

Taking the long perspective on the welfare state in the UK, a trajectory can be seen that starts with the end of the Second World War and the provision by the state of rapidly expanding, formal welfare services as part of the 'social contract' between politicians and citizens throughout the postwar era. Such largely professional and hierarchically organised services, in which citizens were passive recipients and allocated services based on professional assessment, was indeed challenged by the introduction of the 'marketplace' into public services in the context of NPM, which required services users to become consumers and to exercise choice between varieties of providers – be they public, private or not-for-profit agencies. Whatever its drawbacks, one of which was captioned by Lapsley (2009) as being 'the cruellest innovation of the human spirit', NPM at least had the merit of embedding the importance of user choice in the professional and public consciousness.

The present political, 'modernising' agenda (Scottish Government, 2007; Leadbeater and Lownsbrough, 2005) and the emergence of the 'network society' (Hartley, 2005) has shifted the emphasis towards 'consumers' not only having choice in the 'marketplace' but also a 'voice' through New Public Governance (NPG) (Osborne, 2009; 2006). NPG brings a focus on co-producing services in collaboration with public–private networks of resources and services, not simply with individual consumers of the service itself. This trajectory is set out in Table 2.2.

Table 2.2: Trends in policy development.

Ideology	Users	Descriptor
Traditional welfare state	Clients	'On the receiving end'; recipients
NPM; neo-liberalism	Consumers	Active participants; exercising/having choice
NPG; network society	Co-producers	Having a 'voice ' as well as 'choice'; designing, managing as well as consuming; active citizen

Source: Based on Pestoff (2012).

Echoing Leadbeater's (2004) distinction between 'deep' and 'shallow' personalisation, Pestoff (2012) differentiates between co-production 'light' (encompassing interactions between users and the services as they seek to meet their own needs and aspirations) and co-production 'heavy' (characterised by co-governance of services or service commissioning with political implications that he describes as facilitating the 're-democratisation' of the welfare state). It is at the intersection of policies of co-production heavy and the current austerity drive that some of the tensions begin to emerge to which we shall return and consider in greater detail in Chapter 5.

While the introduction of community care legislation in the 1990s resulted in a range of social policies that gradually incorporated discourses of empowerment (see, for example, Taylor *et al.*, 1992), the notion that people who use services have expertise or assets remained visible only on the outside of mainstream policy initiatives. Therefore, while the user engagement agenda has been actively promoted across social work, its relationship has not always been straightforward and has, in turn, reflected a mishmash of user rights alongside managerial and consumerist discourses (Smith *et al.*, 2013). The long campaign for DPs legislation in the UK is a key example of this, where the insights and experiences of disabled people as organisers and employers of their own support required years of campaigning to achieve change. Yet, even when this was set in statute, most local authorities were reluctant to offer DPs as a mainstream social care option (Riddell *et al.*, 2005).

By the mid-2000s, co-production was beginning to emerge more prominently in policy documents within social care, and its appearance in the Department of Health's (2007) *Putting People First* in England and Wales and in *Changing Lives* (Scottish Executive, 2006) in Scotland were among its first outings. Its wide appeal to social care drew on a number of factors. For Hunter and Ritchie (2007), co-production is particularly relevant as an approach: when the situation calls for long-term support; when it is important for support to be highly individualised and 'site specific'; when different people and agencies have to work together; when what is needed is change over time; and when services are likely to have a major rather than minor influence on the person's quality of life.

Issues of equity and social justice

The influence of the disabled people's movement in securing legislation for DPs highlighted a focus on social justice issues in relation to the provision of services (see Chapter 1). However, as discussed so far, there remained both geographical inequity in terms of uptake across the UK (Riddell *et al.*, 2005) and also a concentration of policy access for persons with physical impairments (Witcher *et al.*, 2000). These differences across user groups remained with the implementation of IBs and with early implementation of SDS during the test sites (see chapters 3 and 4 for more detail), in which it was reported that access to IBs for those with mental health problems, older people, those with drug and alcohol problems or from black or minority ethnic groups was not addressed (Ridley *et al.*, 2011). Nor had this changed dramatically overall in the year following the test sites (Ridley *et al.*, 2012).

Yet the inherent flexibility of SDS and its antecedents has appeared to be beneficial for users in more remote parts of Scotland. DPs were initially found to be helpful for people in dispersed rural areas, where traditional services have been more limited (Priestley *et al.*, 2010). Available figures for SDS uptake in Scotland in the form of DPs support these findings and reveal the highest rate of SDS per 10,000 population in the two rural local authorities of Orkney and the Scottish Borders (Scottish Government, 2012). Likewise, other rural authorities such as Shetland and Highland also feature in the 'top ten' local authorities.

While it is now accepted wisdom that public services should be designed to meet user- and community-informed outcomes and not professionally led identification of needs, there are a number of caveats that need to be attached to this. Broader questions surrounding personalisation and social justice have been consistently raised by Ferguson (2012; 2007). He argues that personalisation is a contested concept and, while the values that motivated the independent living movement to pursue DPs are important historically, they tell us little about why personalisation currently takes the form it does. As we explore in Chapter 5, he maintains that personalisation in its current guise is consistent with a neo-liberal social and economic agenda which limits, rather than extends, social justice:

> The construction of personalisation ... as both 'modern' (in the sense of being in tune with the requirements of a globalised world (Harris and White, 2009) and also politically and ethically progressive (in addressing the legitimate demands of users for greater freedom and control) has proved a heady brew. It has resulted in a dominant discourse which presents the paradigm shift to personalisation as being both inevitable and desirable (Ferguson, 2012, p. 61).

Debates around risk
Both carers and professionals have also expressed concern that personalisation and co-production bring with them greater risks than professionally delivered services. While it is apparent that professional services are not without their own risks to users (Flynn, 2012; Francis Report, 2010), Duffy (2010a), for example, argues that the case for the protective factor of family and community involvement is a serious concern that must be recognised as co-production and personalisation are rolled out. As noted by Kinder (2012), there are complexities in servicing vulnerable individuals who are often in unequal power relationships with professionals within the context

of a service framework that assumes their participation and their capacity to participate, and, what is more, they are required to bring their own resources to the table.

Co-production may improve outcomes and user satisfaction for those well able to participate and express their views and preferences, but in order to ensure that everyone can benefit, whatever the degree or nature of vulnerability, additional supports, accessible information and professional time are required to maintain equality of access. In this context, the assertion that 'co-production is value for money but cannot produce value without money' (Bovaird and Loeffler, 2012, p. 1119) seems extremely apt. Otherwise, those individuals and communities with greater material and personal resources will be better placed to pursue their 'outcomes' than some groups with significant vulnerabilities whose circumstances are more hazardous.

Over the last decade, key legislation in Scottish social care such as the Mental Health (Care and Treatment) (Scotland) Act 2003 and the Adults with Incapacity Act 2000 recognised that those least likely to be able to exercise self-determination are most at risk of having their rights ignored. In turn, the role of advocacy – whether self, collective or professional advocacy – has become increasingly important for people requiring access to public services (Donnison, 2009). In Scotland, the approach to advocacy is in itself unique in that it is free, operates nationwide and through an independent service. Prior to implementation, the SDS Bill put a clear focus on individual responsibility for the type of support received, and there were calls for independent advocacy to be included in the legislation as provision under the SDS strategy.

As will be discussed in Chapter 5, the availability of SDS in itself is not a guarantee of choice and control, and other factors such as the size of the allocated budget, availability of other services, advocacy and support are all central components of a successful SDS strategy. The importance of brokerage and support in providing assistance to users of personalised services has been highlighted throughout the respective eras of policy development. This is an equally important consideration in co-production where the queries of commentators as to whether these roles should be undertaken by social workers, who are ultimately accountable to statutory agencies (Barnes and

Mercer, 2006; Pearson, 2004), are even more apposite. Research has also highlighted some antagonism from users to the idea that brokers should be part of the social care workforce at all (Dowson and Greig, 2009). Instead, the role of user-led organisations with peer-led strategies at the heart of their support has been widely accepted as the preferred model of support, and local authorities have been encouraged to adopt this approach (Cabinet Office, 2005). While Centres for Independent/Inclusive Living (CILs) run by disabled people have, in many areas, proved vital in offering this type of role, their levels of support remain uneven. Sadly, the pledge set out in the UK-wide *Improving the Life Chances of Disabled People* (Cabinet Office, 2005) to have a user-led organisation in each local area by 2010 was never realised. Debates around support roles are discussed in more detail in Chapter 4.

It is clear that services are being asked to provide more for, and to work alongside, services users. In consequence, it is anticipated that making better use of each other's assets and resources will achieve enhanced outcomes and efficiency (Governance International, 2011). Unsurprisingly, at a time of reducing public spending, optimism surrounding co-production (with its potential for harnessing community resources) as well as public funding (with its capacity for both producing innovative solutions and drawing on information technology to assist in this) has come into question. In a time of austerity and the deepest economic recession since the Great Depression of the 1930s, questions are inevitably raised about the appropriateness of such policies and expectations in the context of impoverished personal and community resources. As has been said before, however, 'no change' is not an option (Scottish Government, 2010; Scottish Executive, 2006), and therefore those engaged in this work have no choice but to engage with the opportunities offered by these policies while remaining vigilant to the well-catalogued dangers. In Chapter 5 we explore further the tension inherent in implementing SDS and personalisation in a hostile financial climate.

Conclusions

This chapter has explored the key values and themes underpinning SDS. Discussion has documented the meteoric rise of the concept of co-production as the centrepiece of SDS, and has highlighted how values have shifted and how new discourses around user involvement have infiltrated public policy. Critics of personalisation (e.g. Ferguson, 2012) identify this focus on co-production as revealing underlying individualist/consumerist strands at the expense of more communitarian/collective-action-oriented approaches. This clearly limits the potential of SDS to offer greater choice and control in practice – an aspect of policy implementation that we consider further in chapters 3 and 5. Commentary has also examined issues around equality, social justice and risk. This sets the scene for a more detailed focus on the impact of austerity, which will be set out in Chapter 5. Before then, chapters 3 and 4 explore the experiences and views of service professionals involved in front-line and strategic implementation of SDS during the test sites in Scotland.

CHAPTER 3

From Pilot to Mainstream: Drawing on the Experience of Self-directed Support Test Sites in Scotland

Introduction

So far chapters 1 and 2 have described the gradual shift in social care provision towards more personalised approaches in the UK and have introduced key concepts and issues relevant to considering implementation of personalisation and SDS in Scotland. This chapter begins to explore implementation processes and the impact of such transformational changes in social care delivery with reference to empirical studies. In particular, the chapter draws upon findings from evaluation and follow-up studies of three local SDS test sites funded by the Scottish Government, which ran between 2009 and 2011 (Ridley *et al.*, 2012; 2011). Focusing on these findings allows comparison of practice and an opportunity to identify broad lessons for implementation. The studies explore the impact of this 'transformational change' on local authorities and, to some extent, on users, family carers and independent care providers. The chapter also reflects on implementation issues around innovation and co-production emanating from this and other pilots.

As stated in Chapter 1, research to date shows only marginal success for DP policy in Scotland, with many local authorities and social workers remaining reluctant to promote them as a mainstream option, despite early evidence that recipients generally consider the benefits to outweigh by far the challenges (Pearson, 2006; Witcher *et al.*, 2000). Riddell *et al.* (2006) identify several barriers affecting DP implementation including: concerns about the impact on existing provision; inadequate skills development and information for local authority staff; anxieties about financial accountability and cumbersome bureaucracy; concerns about an unregulated workforce; and the influence of micro-cultures on organisational practice and beliefs that inhibit or support the development of DPs. In their analysis of barriers to DPs, Glasby and Littlechild (2009) suggest that social workers' reluctance to engage with them lay in their fundamental unease with the linking of financial and welfare resources in supporting users via DPs. Later studies examining exemplary practice have highlighted the need for: effective support services for DP recipients; effective local authority leadership; 'light touch' more proportionate financial systems; and better training for front-line staff (Homer and Gilder, 2008).

Against this backdrop, in 2009 the Scottish Government sought to embed further the wider policy agendas through the promotion of a framework for SDS. These included strategies for personalisation, social inclusion, participation, empowerment and, as discussed in Chapter 2, co-production (Pestoff, 2012; Scottish Government, 2010; Hunter and Ritchie, 2007; Scottish Executive, 2006). Up until 2010, Scotland had lagged behind the rest of the UK in rolling out personalisation, and DP rates have remained lower than England (Dunning, 2010). As set out in Chapter 1, this was to change with the Scottish Government launch of a ten-year strategy with COSLA making SDS 'the mainstream mechanism for the delivery of social care' to transform the way social care is delivered throughout Scotland (Scottish Government, 2010). To recap, this was backed by significant 'transformation investment' in local authorities to help them implement SDS: £3.6 million supporting the creation of three SDS test sites between 2009 and 2011, and £25 million to support local authority developments between 2011 and 2015. In addition, the Scottish Government also invested in user and support projects developments; in provider capacity-building; and workforce change. Implementation of the 2013 Act in April 2014 obliged local authorities to offer SDS, thus henceforth making this the mandatory approach to social care in Scotland.

Personalisation has been called a 'transformative agenda' by government, requiring fundamental change in the funding of social care, the workforce and local authorities as well as for users (Beresford, 2009; HM Government, 2007). Responses from Scottish local authorities on implementation plans confirm this, with the majority identifying the need for system-wide and organisational culture change (Self-directed Support Scotland, 2013). Powell (2012) sets out a number of implications for the social care workforce and for local authorities attempting to implement personalisation. These include: the need for professionals to find new collaborative ways of working and developing local partnerships with users; tailoring support to meet individual needs; recognising and supporting carers; access to universal community services and resources; and focusing on early intervention and prevention. This chapter reflects on the extent to which such challenges were highlighted and met by Self-directed Support Scotland (SDSS) test sites and other pilots, and considers the impact on systems of service delivery. Workforce issues and the impact on support roles are the focus of Chapter 4. Also, while this chapter makes passing reference to the wider context of the impact of austerity measures and budget cuts on SDS implementation, this is considered more fully in Chapter 5.

The chapter starts by discussing the slippery and evolving concept of SDS and how this played out in the Scottish SDS test sites. It then looks at: the impact of the test sites' attempts to shift from traditional service provision to an approach better able to meet individuals' aspirations; their experience of developing more transparent systems for the allocation of resources on an individual basis; and the change towards using a self-assessment system and adopting outcomes-based planning approaches. The discussion considers broader issues of user involvement in the strategic implementation of SDS, and reflects upon the impact of the pace of change on the effectiveness of implementation.

The pilot sites

In 2009, as government cuts on social welfare spending were just beginning to impact, the Scottish Government in collaboration with COSLA selected three local authorities to act as test sites for SDS implementation and awarded each a grant of £1.2 million over two years. The test sites were to address three main issues that it identified from research: the importance of leadership and training; the need to reduce bureaucracy or 'red tape'; and the need for bridging finance to double fund existing services while introducing more individualised models of support. In large part, the three local authorities had flexibility over how they operationalised being a test site, including deciding the focus of attention, and they had additional resources to implement new systems through the Scottish Government grant, as well as control over the pace of implementation. This was to change over the period of the test sites as major reform of community care legislation gathered pace, increasing the obligation on all Scottish local authorities to implement SDS as the mainstream approach in the context of ever-shrinking resources.

Test site 1

Dumfries & Galloway is in a rural part of Scotland. When it became a test site, the local authority was already working towards transforming its approach to social care delivery to embrace the broader personalisation agenda and testing out the application of an *In Control* approach (see Chapter 1 for more details) in a rural setting and across client groups. As well as developing appropriate systems for SDS, the council emphasised preventative and early intervention support, and community capacity-building as part of an overall personalisation strategy. Expressly not wanting to implement personalisation as a top-down policy, the Dumfries & Galloway test site took a more gradualist approach or what was described as a 'community development approach', initially working with small numbers of users and carers from one geographical area, aiming to promote personalisation from the bottom up and build staff confidence in implementing new models.

Test site 2

In contrast, test site 2 (Glasgow) is the largest urban authority in Scotland and the local authority decided to use the opportunity of becoming a test site to build directly upon its IB pilot that had run in the east of the city, aiming to achieve more personalised support specifically for people with learning difficulties. During the test site period, it aimed to increase the number of IBs and, wherever possible, significantly to increase the uptake of DPs. To begin with, systems of self-assessment and RAS were adapted from the *In Control* model of SDS and applied to practise with small numbers of users. As the test site progressed, both the target group and the numbers of SDS recipients expanded dramatically as a major, top-down phased programme for SDS was implemented. Partnership working with service providers and others was an explicit and key element of Glasgow's approach.

Test site 3
Highland is a remote rural authority in Scotland, which initially set out to promote SDS through increasing the number of people accessing DPs. However, it did so by developing a parallel system from an existing DP scheme. As with the other test sites, Highland Council was keen to implement the *In Control* model of SDS, except in the method used to determine the size of IBs and allocate resources. Different from the other two pilots, which implemented RAS, was the fact that Highland Council trialled a 'service equivalency' model – that is, arriving at a figure equivalent to what would have been spent on traditional services. In this area, young people in transition into adult services and those with learning difficulties and/or autism became the main target groups, though in practice one-off payments were made to a wider range of client groups than this throughout the two years of the test site.

SDS as an evolving concept
Unlike DPs, which an individual does or does not receive, SDS has proven to be a more nebulous concept. In recent years, there has been an identified shift in the official rhetoric about personalisation: changing from one primarily about offering individuals control over budgets, to more generally emphasising the importance of offering 'choice and control' and focusing on outcomes (Beresford, 2009). The experience of the SDS test sites demonstrates a similar evolution of the SDS concept in Scotland. At inception, the Scottish Government stated a key goal of the test sites was to increase the number and range of people with DPs, referring to SDS and DPs interchangeably: 'The very baseline is Manifesto commitments, each of the test

sites must demonstrate increase in take-up of direct payments as an absolute ...' (interview with Scottish Government SDS Team).

Up until 2013 this focus was reflected in national data collection across Scottish councils – *Self-directed Support (Direct Payments)* (Self-directed Support Scotland, 2013) – though, since 2011, the Health Analytical Services Division has been working with councils on ways to broaden data capture to encompass the range of SDS options beyond DPs alone. The consensus of opinion across different local and national stakeholders, however, was that SDS refers to a spectrum of options with DPs at one end and individually tailored, local authority-provided services at the other. While some users would choose directly to control the budget allocated and employ his/her own staff using a DP, others might instead choose to:

> Co-design the service, to talk about what kind of outcomes they want to achieve from the service, what they want their lives to be like – and they have a pretty good say then in how the resources for that service are directed (national provider).

Prior to the test sites, informants from the local areas and national user and professional organisations that were interviewed highlighted a number of flaws in established DP systems, not least that they had become overly prescriptive, bureaucratic and used 'old style' care management processes. Ironically, DPs were said in practice to be restrictive, inflexible and focused on specified outputs. In contrast, with its focus on outcomes and co-production, SDS was understood to have the potential to offer greater freedom for individuals to decide their support arrangements, including the option to go for in-house services as well as DPs. In this respect, SDS had the potential to address the perceived shortcomings of DPs and radically to change the face of social care delivery.

In all three SDS test sites there was a paradox at the heart of the process: the research consistently found a (mis)perception by staff, users and carers of SDS as an alternative not only to managed or direct services but also to DPs. Consequently, rather than existing DP systems offering a starting point for the development of SDS, new and parallel administrative systems for SDS – including offering a cash payment – were set up. Later on, there were subsequent attempts to integrate these parallel systems of SDS and DPs. This distinction between the two systems continued throughout the life of the test sites, with some users and carers reporting having both a DP and a cash payment under the banner of SDS – a situation that was understandably confusing for local authority staff, users and carers alike.

As mentioned in Chapter 1, the *National Strategy* (Scottish Government, 2010), and subsequent 2013 Act, adopted far broader definitions of SDS, with DPs as just one mechanism for delivery. SDSS on its website describes SDS as giving people: 'a range of options about how their social care is delivered, beyond just DPs, empowering people to decide how much ongoing control and responsibility they want over their own support arrangements'. The four options on how social care can be delivered under the 2013 Act are set out in Chapter 2. To recap these include: (1) a DP; (2) the person directs the available support; (3) the local authority arranges the support; or (4) a mix of these three options. The key requirements, regardless of the mechanism used to deliver support, are the exercise of choice and control, and co-production. The range of support packages evidenced during the SDS test sites were reflective of this broad definition and the four options, which included DPs as well as individually tailored local authority services. A lack of precision in defining SDS was, however, commented upon negatively by user organisations. For example, one said:

> I despair about the terminology, it is muddled and confusing. The Bill defined four ways that SDS can be implemented – via DP; IB; 'just provide my service please', i.e., service agreement; or a mixture of the first three. So almost anything can be SDS.

Although during the test sites DP was the most common SDS option – four out of five SDS packages involved a DP either to an individual or third party – this was not the case by the time of the follow-up study undertaken one year after the test sites (Ridley *et al.*, 2012). The phased implementation programme introduced by Glasgow resulted in a major shift occurring towards local authority-arranged support packages, so much so that this option had increased from a third to 96% of Glasgow's SDS packages. By this point, many of the SDS packages in Glasgow involved a mix of the four options outlined earlier, with just under half also receiving a DP. Post the test-site period, local authority-arranged support remained in the minority in the other two sites, with all those in the SDS programme in Highland receiving a DP, and around 90% of those in Dumfries & Galloway doing so.

While the picture that emerged during the test sites should not be assumed to describe current developments in SDS across Scotland, it is interesting that, similar to the Glasgow experience, recent studies of personal and health budgets in England found the majority of personalisation packages were arranged and managed by local authorities (Beresford, 2013; Slasberg *et al.*, 2013; ADASS, 2011). The ADASS survey (2011) confirms that, although the number of people with PBs increased significantly in England, nearly all of this rise was in the form of council-managed budgets, thereby sparking concern that some councils were allocating nominal PBs without offering people real choice and control (Slasberg *et al.*, 2013).

Trials and tribulations of individual budgets
IBs, as discussed in chapters 1 and 2, represented a radical departure from providing services to allocating a sum of money to those eligible for social care services to determine for themselves how their care needs should be met (Department of Health, 2006). This differs from DP in that it refers essentially to the allocation of a budget, not to how this will be managed, whereas a DP is a cash transfer to an individual or third party for them to meet their care needs. As Glasby and Duffy (2007) explain, an IB is about 'being clear with people from day one how much is available to spend on meeting their needs', then ensuring they have as much control and choice over how this is spent. Although the rhetoric of IBs is powerful, the speed of implementation nationally was, as Carr (2013) observes, made on the basis of extremely limited evidence from small pilot projects.

In Scotland, results from a small-scale demonstration project in North Lanarkshire were positive about the benefits of IBs (see Chapter 2) and the potential of the *In Control* approach (Etherington *et al.*, 2009). Findings from the only large-scale study of IBs in England

(Glendinning *et al.*, 2008), however, paint a more complex picture, and point to a number of implementation issues requiring further examination (Beresford, 2013). Since then, conclusions from the national PB surveys in England (Hatton and Waters, 2013) – attributing positive benefits to the impact of PBs – have been challenged on the basis that this fails to take into account that the vast majority of PBs were taken as a DP (Slasberg *et al.*, 2013). Furthermore, those who received services from their council did not experience the same positive outcomes. In light of this and the level of council-managed services reported in the test sites' follow-up study, it would be misleading to read the introduction of IBs or PBs as equating with increased choice and control in social care.

The experience of the Dumfries & Galloway test site throws into question whether or not 'upfront' budget allocations are helpful. While accepting that the resource allocation in the form of an IB should be transparent and 'upfront' (Mind, 2009), the Personalisation Team in Dumfries & Galloway test site conclude that such transparency sometimes resulted in inferior solutions being proposed to meet individuals' needs as the focus shifted to the budget entitlement rather than the outcomes sought. They emphasise that it was more important to identify and work with natural supports in the person's network to develop creative solutions before a budget figure was introduced so as not to inhibit thinking about potential solutions:

> The *In Control* 7-steps didn't work for us. It was the money upfront bit. What we learnt from the test site was that if you tell people what the money is you get a plan that is that to the penny. We did a few where we didn't say what the indicative budget was and quite a few came in at less and they were more outcomes focused. Giving the figure upfront we found was skewing people's thinking, and the plans were not quite as creative (Personalisation Team, Dumfries & Galloway).

Furthermore, Dumfries & Galloway subsequently invented three more stages to *In Control*'s seven-step approach, effectively introducing the indicative budget later in the process.

As in the PB pilots evaluation (Hatton and Waters, 2013), user and carer satisfaction with SDS during the test sites was associated, among other things, with agreement about the panel's decision on the size of the IB in relation to what they identified was needed. Indeed, where users and carers did express dissatisfaction with SDS, commonly this was with a discrepancy between what they perceived as their needs and the eventual financial allocation, as well as with differences in perceptions of need. At times, engaging with SDS resulted in users feeling they had been encouraged to have 'false expectations' as one disabled man suggests:

> They seemed quite in agreement with what we needed and what we had self-assessed and then, as I say, it [the Support Plan] went away and sat in front of this Board and when we got word back everything had been cut ...

As we predict in Chapter 5, such dissatisfaction with SDS budget allocations is likely to grow in future, given the financial constraints that local authorities increasingly face.

Ongoing challenges with resource allocation

An RAS is defined as 'a set of rules that can be used to calculate an IB' (Duffy, 2010a, p. 4). The test sites adopted different models for deciding budget allocations, though all set up panels of some kind. Their experiences demonstrate fundamental problems with these systems. One user-led organisation commented: 'Looking back I feel we [disabled people's movement] fought for SDS and personalisation, but not for the RAS.'

Implementing the *In Control* RAS proved highly time-consuming, and the application of formulas designed for use with people with learning difficulties were found to be inadequate when it was necessary to make decisions about the size of IB needed by individuals from other client groups. Challenges with allocating resources fairly persisted long after the test sites ended. As one SDS test site lead officer reflected:

> Getting the resource allocation right is an art not a system – it needs to be flexible. Slotting people into boxes is not going to work. At the end of the test site and now there is still a need to develop an equitable way of distributing and

managing resources. We know what we have is not quite right but we haven't solved this issue yet.

By the follow-up evaluation, all three areas had shifted from central to local decision-making panels, and Glasgow had also created 'risk enablement panels' to deal with complex or challenging decisions. At the end of the test site, Highland Council decided to abandon the 'service equivalency' model, as defined earlier, which it had used rather than a RAS, while Glasgow and Dumfries & Galloway continued to grapple with refinements to RAS-based systems:

> We started off using the RAS but we found that it did not work to use this in a rigid way and there needed to be dialogue to shape the process. It can take a long time to budget appropriately, particularly if you are trying to be clear and transparent (key stakeholder, Dumfries & Galloway).

As we discuss further in Chapter 5, recent research highlights a major discrepancy between budget figures arrived at during assessment compared with the final budget agreed by RAS panels, with commentators concluding that SDS is failing to deliver on either PBs or personalisation (Slasberg et al., 2013). Series and Clements (2013) find a similar disparity between indicative and final budget figures as decided by RAS. While the test site numbers were small and do not provide exact comparative data, participants' comments overall indicate that similar concerns are emerging in Scotland, despite some care managers suggesting that panels in their area tended to approve the requested budgets: 'My experience at panel has been that if the plan sets out good outcomes and there is evidence of co-production then the plan will be approved' (survey respondent).

In the follow-up study, a majority of study participants in Glasgow commented that actual budget levels were invariably lower than proposed levels, and it could appear to users that their support was being cut – around three out of five care managers agreed that SDS budgets were insufficient to meet needs. This is similar to the national Community Care and Unison (2011) PBs survey, which found that 48% of social work practitioners surveyed thought PBs were insufficient to meet users' needs. A more encouraging picture emerged from the Dumfries & Galloway test site, where care managers commonly agreed that allocated budgets were sufficient to meet assessed needs. The Personalisation Team, however, expressed concern that the overarching focus on saving money within the authority would inevitably negatively impact in the future. While many care managers in Highland felt unable to give an opinion regarding budget levels because SDS systems were at an early stage of development there, some of those who responded agreed that allocated budgets were sufficient to meet needs. Nonetheless, in Highland among those interviewed as well as respondents to the care managers' survey, disquiet was expressed regarding budget constraints, making it difficult to get funding approval for more 'aspirational' rather than 'critical' needs. Moreover, a few survey respondents referred to a problem of 'top slicing 20%' from requested budgets to make savings. These findings are ironic given personalisation was initially promoted as being aspirational (Needham, 2011b).

All in all, the experience of the test sites suggests that RAS are in need of further refinement. The issues experienced chime with the apology for creating RAS given by Duffy in 2012, in which he suggests that systems had become needlessly complex when they should be simple. As Stack (2013) observes, the reality of RAS is 'a more opaque system' than that intended. However, Slasberg *et al.* (2013) argue that the root of the problem actually lies more fundamentally in what is meant by a 'fair allocation'. As we further discuss in Chapter 6, research evidence suggests that RAS is far from transparent, and those implementing SDS continue to face a number of thorny issues – not least that such systems have had a tendency to become heavily bureaucratic and cannot be immune to cuts in public services (Beresford, 2013). Other studies found that RAS is poorly understood (London SDS Forum, 2013). The test sites worked hard to find ways to make the decision-making processes for allocating IBs work across urban, rural and remote rural areas, but the challenges remained one year on from the test sites.

Experiences of implementing processes of self-assessment
National guidance from the Scottish Government on SDS published in 2007 advocated self-assessment processes to ensure individuals

are involved in considerations about their needs. Indeed, self-assessment is a core element of the *In Control* model adopted by the test sites, whereby (in theory) an individual is helped to complete a self-assessment process that is then used to inform the allocation of an indicative budget. The early stages of the journey towards personalisation in South Lanarkshire reinforced the need for the individual to set their own goals and for support to be shaped around these, and for professionals to find new ways of working in co-production with users to achieve this (Kettle *et al.*, 2011). Specialist SDS or personalisation teams in the test sites concentrated much of their time designing specific SDS assessment protocols and processes that aimed for greater user involvement (Ridley *et al.*, 2011). In 2009, however, ADASS identified the notion of self-assessment as problematic in that it disregards the legal duty of the local authority to take assessment decisions. In the test sites, as elsewhere (Department of Health, 2008), therefore, the notion of supported self-assessment evolved whereby users have the lead in identifying their needs and their preferred ways of meeting them while local authorities retain control of eligibility and support planning decisions (Leece and Leece, 2011).

Assessment during the SDS test sites took varying lengths of time from one or two short visits from an assessor (not necessarily a care manager) culminating in a written care plan that users and carers were asked to agree with, to others involving far lengthier processes over several months. For example, a care manager describes an SDS assessment process he was involved with as taking over six months:

> It's a process people have to engage in. They have to understand that and that takes some time to explain … It took us quite a long while to actually get Tom's plan written or to get Tom to write the plan … (Care manager) (name of user anonymised).

During the test sites evaluation, levels of user and carer satisfaction with involvement in the assessment processes were high among the sample of thirty people whose experiences featured as in-depth case studies. This contrasted with the survey of PB practitioners by the London SDS Forum (2013) in which most front-line workers said that users did not understand SDS, and did not think new systems of assessment ensured more choice and control. Although meant to give users a much bigger say, Stack (2013) argues supported self-assessment has often proved in practice to be an 'unwieldy questionnaire with tick boxes that fail to "individualise" the service user's needs'. Users and carers in the test sites generally said they had had an opportunity to say what they wanted or that the needs of the person they cared for had been properly considered. Other research has suggested that self-assessment can lead to under-assessing need (Rabiee *et al.*, 2009).

Only a minority of people interviewed during the test sites felt that assessors did not consult with those who knew the person well. Differences between good and poor involvement in assessment were attributed to individual care manager's attitudes about the importance of co-production. One user, who said they felt sufficiently involved, still lacked ownership of a plan that had effectively been created by a professional conducting the assessment: 'Most of what's on that sheet I didn't suggest it, it was them (the assessor) that wrote it.'

The care manager in this situation, who at the time of the test sites had not received training in the new assessment process, was unsure about the SDS paperwork and how to put a good case together for the panel. Despite this lack of involvement, the user reported being pleased with the outcome. In contrast, another care manager from the same test site, who had worked with a man with learning disabilities, demonstrated the importance of using more creative ways of engaging people and what co-production and self-assessment should mean. The plan he referred to was written as a 'kind of narrative', with the process simplified, making it easier for the user to understand. Such an approach echoes the Personal Outcomes Approach advocated by the Joint Improvement Team (Cook and Miller, 2012), emphasising the importance of a negotiation in working through complex circumstances to arrive at a person-centred support plan based on the person's priorities.

Some users and carers in the test sites questioned the relevance of their involvement in assessment in light of unfavourable resource panel decisions. How meaningful a term self-assessment, even supported self-assessment, was to describe what happened in practice during the test sites was questionable: the great majority of SDS assessments were completed by professionals, with the main contributors being the person's relatives:

> It was out of his hands and he just kind of agreed to it but … I don't think he made a decision really himself but she [autism nurse] certainly explained it to him what's going to happen … I think decision-making is quite hard for him … he's not quite sure exactly what he needs at times (parent of young man with autism).

A social worker from a different test site reflected further that there are 'huge issues' regarding involvement in assessment, particularly for people with learning difficulties and/or complex needs. Despite steps being taken to ensure an individual's needs and wants were identified and considered, she commented that 'it is not a fully self-directed assessment'. Pile (2013) highlights ethical issues arising from documentation purporting to be written in the first person, whether or not the person has capacity issues. There was limited evidence that the test sites had used innovative approaches to support decision-making or had ensured independent advocacy provision for users with less capacity (Edge, 2001). Even one year on, at the follow-up evaluation period, access to advocacy was uneven. Where independent advocates had been involved in supporting individuals in the assessment process, however, this was positively reported.

Alongside SDS assessments, single shared assessment processes were also in use during the test sites, which created additional tiers of form filling. Some care managers commented that this made the assessment process all the more thorough, while others resented what they saw as duplication of paperwork and the extra bureaucracy surrounding SDS, even though they also said the self-assessment tools developed were 'ideal if the time is available'.

Conclusions

Much has been said about the 'transformational' and radical potential of personalisation and SDS to increase individuals' choice and control of their social care, but as Beresford (2013) claims – and would seem to be borne out by the research discussed in this chapter

– the reality may be more disappointing. The experience of Scotland's SDS test sites alongside that of other pilots indicate that implementation has been, and remains, challenging, and that the pace of change has been slow, except in Glasgow. In that city, a major programme to mainstream SDS implementation post test site was introduced, with major consequences for the confidence of users and carers, and the morale of the social services workforce. Development of policy and practice of this magnitude of necessity takes time, and investment in infrastructure for implementation may not translate into outcomes for large numbers of individuals in the short term. Local authorities across Scotland acknowledge that change has to address organisational culture and the barriers to SDS, as well as being system wide (Self-directed Support Scotland, 2013).

Offering people an individual budgetary allocation and giving them the opportunity to say how this should be spent to meet their care needs may seem simple but is a radical departure from traditional service culture. Despite the powerful rhetoric surrounding IBs, the discrepancies in the size of budgetary allocations found by several research studies, including the test sites, throws into question its usefulness as a proxy indicator of choice and control. Implementation of SDS clearly raises a number of ongoing challenges for local authorities and front-line staff. The research evidence to date suggests that some of these challenges, such as finding suitable RAS, remain problematic. The reality of self-assessment is that, without concomitant provision being made for supported decision-making, those who lack capacity or have challenging communication are effectively excluded. The lack of investment in independent advocacy during the test sites meant that those with more challenging support needs were excluded from the process of assessment.

With decreasing resources for social care, it is unclear how the limited, but nonetheless, important innovations reported in the SDS test sites and IB pilots will be sustained. Few of those in the personal health budgets pilot (Davidson *et al.*, 2012) were clear about the future of their budget beyond the first year. In the test sites, only in Dumfries & Galloway were the majority of personalisation or SDS packages set up during the test site period still in place one year later. While this situation requires more detailed investigation, it does raise questions about whether, and the extent to which, the support that was highly valued by users and carers during piloting SDS is sustainable and can be replicated as SDS is mainstreamed across Scotland and out of the spotlight of specific grant-funded initiatives.

CHAPTER 4

Reflections on the Transformational Impact of Self-directed Support on Support Roles

Introduction

In Chapter 3, the focus of discussion around implementation was the transformation of local authority systems to facilitate SDS. This highlighted particular challenges arising during the SDS test sites in Scotland and other pilots in the UK when working with IBs and other self-assessment systems, and when applying RAS in different contexts. We now consider the impact of SDS implementation on support roles, including the implications for training and development of social workers and care managers. The potential of the SDS and personalisation agenda radically to transform the nature of social services has been viewed optimistically by some as presenting an opportunity to move away from the gatekeeping role of care management and to enable social workers to engage more with individual casework. Others, however, argue that it increases bureaucracy and undermines social work and public provision, as well as social care organisations' capacity to deliver person-centred support. In this chapter, we discuss such issues with reference to findings from a survey of care managers conducted in the follow-up evaluation of the test sites (Ridley *et al.*, 2012) alongside other research to reflect upon the potential future implications for support roles as SDS becomes increasingly formalised in the Scottish social care system.

Many commentators have suggested that the changes envisaged in implementing personalisation and SDS will transform all levels of interaction. In the words of the Association of Directors of Social

Work (ADSW, 2009, p. 3), this will 'depend upon a re-framing of social care and corporate practice, commissioning and service delivery'. Furthermore, the ramifications for support apply as much to services delivered by the voluntary and private sectors as to local authority services: Cunningham and Nickson (2011), for example, identify significant changes emerging for voluntary sector recruitment and human resources policy and practice. Even so, as Lymbery and Morley (2012) comment in relation to policy documents, the implications for social work remain sketchy. In setting out a broad agenda for change to implement personalisation, the *Changing Lives* review of social work (Scottish Executive, 2006) identifies the necessity for front-line practitioners to increase their skills in working alongside and building capacity in individuals, families and communities.

Training was a key area considered by the SDS test sites who received a grant over two years to trial work around three themes, which included leadership and training, and since then all Scottish local authorities implementing the 2013 Act have reported introducing major programmes of staff training for SDS (Self-directed Support Scotland, 2013). This chapter first considers user involvement in relation to the strategic development and planning around SDS implementation, and moves on to discuss the implications arising from putting into practice more personalised support and co-produced assessment and support planning. We look critically at issues of commissioning and micro-provision by examining local authorities' attempts to meet the extensive training and development needs of the social care workforce, and at issues of regulation and the interface of adult protection and SDS agendas.

User involvement in SDS implementation

Government and user organisations alike have emphasised the importance of support organisations as critical to successful implementation of DP policy (Pearson, 2006). The centrality of support schemes, especially of user-led support schemes, in increasing the uptake of DPs and achieving the goals of the independent living movement are confirmed by research (Barnes and Mercer, 2006; Riddell *et al.*, 2005). As documented throughout this book, however, while the role of disability activism was central to the expansion of

DPs, the development of user-led support organisations across the UK has been rather more patchy, with a reluctance among many local authorities to fund organisations such as the CILs beyond their role in providing supporting to DP recipients (Pearson, 2006). A study exploring the capacity of disabled people's organisations in Scotland to engage and influence public authorities concludes that there is a need for staff training in both public authorities and disability organisations, and for public authorities to support disability organisations better, to enable them to engage (Johnston and Quarriers, 2009). The importance of involving user organisations in the strategic planning and development of SDS therefore seems beyond question. Nevertheless, as Beresford (2009) suggests, one of the ironies of personalisation is that users and their organisations have had limited say in its planning, development or strategic implementation (see also Carr, 2011; Boxall *et al.*, 2009). The perception among some user and professional organisations in Scotland interviewed in 2009 to establish a baseline for the SDS test sites evaluation was of SDS as a 'professionally driven' agenda (Ridley *et al.*, 2011). As one representative of a national interest group commented: 'The whole thing is being confused by different models being developed without the involvement of disabled people.'

Another national provider of social care argued that 'there is not a huge groundswell for DPs in mental health' and that pressure to increase uptake had not originated from users, at least not from mental health service users. Inadequate or non-existent support infrastructures for users and carers wanting to consider DPs was identified by these respondents as a major obstacle to increasing the future uptake of SDS. While CILs are usually viewed by disabled people's organisations as central to the success of independent living initiatives (Barnes and Mercer, 2006; Cabinet Office, 2005), at the beginning of the test sites there were only two such organisations in Scotland (one each in Edinburgh and Glasgow), together with the Scottish Personal Assistants Employers Network (SPAEN) offering independent, user-led support. There were small, local, independent support agencies in other parts of Scotland, although they were often perceived as disadvantaged in the current commissioning and financial environment.

During the test sites, there was no evidence of local authorities investing either in capacity-building of disabled people's organisa-tions that could offer user-led support on SDS/DPs, or in independent advocacy to support individuals throughout the SDS process. This was the case despite consensus at the start of the test sites that independ-ent support for people who wanted to take up a DP, for instance, was inadequate, with existing support organisations described as 'fragile'. The study of disability organisations in Scotland by Johnston and Quarriers (2009) reiterates that a proactive approach to user engage-ment is critical. Interviews with representatives of both user and carer organisations at Stages 1 and 2 of the test sites evaluation (where these could be identified) indicate only peripheral, if any, involvement of users and carers in developing test site action plans. One year after the test sites, there was evidence of national, though not local, invest-ment in user-led support and independent advocacy to develop SDS. Given that citizen leadership and co-production, at both individual and strategic level, are central to the values and principles of SDS, this is a crucial omission. As Rummery *et al.* (2012) argue, unless advocacy and support organisations play a significant role, it is likely that only the more articulate and well-informed users (or those with advocates and/or support) will be able to secure high-quality services at reduced cost. The recent report from the Equality and Human Rights Commission (cited in Ferguson, 2012, p. 65) concludes that a shift towards PBs without support for independent advocacy will only widen inequalities.

Implementing personalised support

Policy documents in Scotland and the UK (Scottish Government, 2010; Department of Health, 2008; Scottish Executive, 2006) acknowledge that the reform of public services through personalisa-tion and SDS will require a radically altered social services workforce able to deliver person-centred support. Beresford (2013) argues that the way forward lies in implementing 'true person-centred support'. As Renshaw (2008) states, to achieve transformational change and implement personalisation, social workers need to work alongside disabled people rather than *for* disabled people. One personalisation lead in the Dumfries & Galloway test site reflects this perspective:

The change that's involved is cultural rather than system change. How do we get people past thinking it's only about money? We get queries from practitioners about policies, forms and systems but our main focus we feel is on changing the mindset. It's about radically shifting the power balance in the support relationship.

In mental health this means not only fundamental change in the role of mental health services, but also meeting cultural and attitudinal challenges within its workforce (Young, 2010; Bamber and Flanagan, 2008). Findings from the English study of IB pilots (Glendinning *et al.*, 2008) show that the majority of people chose to manage their budget as a DP. Those at the front line of rolling out SDS will therefore need to understand, and be knowledgeable about, how to access DPs, especially as under the new SDS Act, introduced into Scotland in April 2014, DP was one of the four options that can be chosen (see Chapter 2).

A number of challenges for the social worker role have been identified (Leece and Leece, 2011; Newbronner *et al.*, 2011; Manthorpe *et al.*, 2010b). Despite strong argument for the importance of the social work role in SDS and personalisation (e.g. Scottish Executive, 2006), evidence is cited of local authorities reducing the number of social workers in response to major public sector cuts (Lymbery and Morley, 2012). In *Changing Lives* (Scottish Executive, 2006), greater flexibility in the social work role was envisaged, and a need to enhance the capacity of the wider social services workforce to work alongside and engage users, families and communities. Since the emergence of DP legislation from the late 1990s, there has been an ongoing debate relating to the role of social workers as 'gatekeepers' to services, which in some cases has restricted access to these types of schemes (see, for example, Priestley *et al.*, 2010). Disabled people have also expressed concern over prejudicial attitudes towards some user groups and a perception that some – for example, those with fluctuating mental health conditions – would not be able to manage DPs (Ridley, 2006).

Resistance to change in some areas has been based on concerns from front-line staff over the impact of personalised support on the statutory workforce (Priestley *et al.*, 2010; Pearson, 2004). Indeed, processes of self-assessment as developed by *In Control* (Etherington *et al.*, 2009) and *Talking Points* in Scotland (Cook and Miller, 2012) require marked shifts in both the 'expert' culture and mindset of professionals, as well as in the commissioning of services geared to meeting outcomes. The implications for training and developing the social care workforce cannot be underestimated. Wider issues are also raised for social work practitioners about the role of support and/or service brokerage in promoting SDS options. Official statements suggest that social workers will be expected to spend less time on assessment and gatekeeping, and instead be involved with support brokerage and advocacy (HM Government, 2007; Department of Health, 2008). Nevertheless, although both advocacy and brokerage resonate with the ethos of social work, the need for these to be independent of service provision does not (Leece and Leece, 2011). Indeed, research has found unease among users and carers to the idea of brokers being part of the social care workforce (Dowson and Greig, 2009). Furthermore, Gardner (2011) suggests it is unclear at this stage whether or not support brokerage is a direct threat to the social work role. Interestingly, none of the three SDS test sites chose to develop the support brokerage model.

It has also been argued that personalisation is an opportunity for practitioners to return to traditional social work values and ways of working (Kettle *et al.*, 2011). Indeed, earlier research concerned with defining person-centred support underlined the importance of core values, and of training for front-line workers to increase their confidence to work in co-production with users (Glynn *et al.*, 2008). As Carr (2010, p. 16) suggests, placing the individual at the centre, having respect for the individual and the value of self-determination are 'at the heart of social work' and constitute 'good social work practice'. Duffy (2007) claims 'strong congruence' between SDS and core social work values, while also suggesting that the care management function may need to shift radically from assessment towards review, and towards intensive support for some, moving from a deficit to capacity mode of thinking. SDS leads in the Scottish Government commented:

> From people that we've spoken to who've been fairly Senior Directors of the service, Heads of Service, they want

assessment to get back to basics and to allow Care Managers and Social Workers to return to key values, that is, what their key role should be is helping people to direct their own support.

Yet, as Leece and Leece (2011) argue, few social workers will have experience of a therapeutic approach in the current assessment and care management model. They need a 'new script' (as suggested by Leadbeater, 2004) in order to move out of the technical and procedural patterns of working as care managers (Duffy, 2010a).

As the Individual Budgets Evaluation Network (IBSEN) study (Glendinning *et al.*, 2008) found, social workers and care co-ordinators/care managers differ in the extent to which the shift to IBs has given them the opportunity to rediscover traditional social work skills. Furthermore, as Young (2010, p. 316) argues, many of those in support roles will have to 'undergo a change of mindset' fully to embrace new ways of working, and the shift in the locus of power inherent in the SDS framework. It was proposed by Duffy (2010b) that social workers should embrace personalisation as consonant with both the ideologies of self-determination and choice, and with good practice 'technologies' such as person-centred planning. Others (Ferguson, 2012; Scourfield, 2005) have been more critical, suggesting that social workers could find themselves in a position of bad faith, implementing a policy that intentionally or otherwise might be perceived by users and carers as a device for cutting services. How social workers, individually and as a profession, respond, are managed and are trained to respond in front-line practice will be a persistent challenge. Despite a heavy investment in extensive training and awareness-raising programmes for front-line workers by the SDS test sites, one year on we found a high proportion of care managers across the three areas remained dissatisfied with the training and guidance they had received on how to implement SDS (Ridley *et al.*, 2012). As one care manager commented, encouragement to change practice needs to amount to more than 'hectoring individual social workers to be more imaginative and risk-enabling'.

Assessment, outcomes and co-production

Central to the SDS system is that assessment is led by a consideration of outcomes, identified by the user themselves and their preferred way of meeting them (Miller, 2012). A significant proportion of the time spent developing new systems in the SDS test sites was spent on developing systems of assessment, and this is considered more extensively in Chapter 3. The approach is characterised by a belief that individuals are 'expert' in their own problems and, furthermore, have assets and skills that they can bring to bear on their resolution alongside public service resources (Evans, 2012). This stands in contrast to traditional deficit planning associated with needs-led assessment and which is typically professional led. It is underlined within the SDS process by the emphasis on co-production and collective agreement. Key stakeholders interviewed for the follow-up evaluation in all three test sites framed the main issue as being about supporting a radical cultural shift in the power relationship between professionals and users, and not simply dealing with technological fixes or designing the right forms and processes. Facilitating and supporting users to identify and articulate their needs, and to develop personalised support plans, require social workers to redefine their expertise and professional role (Gardner, 2011). This was such an thorny issue that, in the year following the SDS test sites, areas continued to develop and refine their assessment processes, with one setting up a short-life working group involving service users and carers.

Although local authorities retain control of eligibility and support planning decisions, the focus on co-production is clearly a significant change to the roles and tasks of social work. Support for users to plan their care can come from a range of sources not only social workers but also family and friends, service brokers, community groups or user-led organisations can be involved (Evans, 2012). Rabiee (2012), for example, argues that practitioners will be required to have a more nuanced understanding of users' concept of independence. From her longitudinal work with disabled people and older people, she suggests that independence is 'highly relative, conditional and multidimensional' and not "fixed" or "given" ' (Rabiee, 2012, p. 877). In a personalised system, an assessment based on a professional's definition of needs becomes an obstacle to individual choice and control

(Foster *et al.*, 2006). Rabiee (2012) argues it is crucial for social work practice therefore that assessments and responses to needs are timely, flexible and based on individual circumstances and not determined by the priorities of existing services. Evans (2012) proffers an example of student placements within disabled people's organisations as having the potential to change power dynamics radically in line with the ethos of personalisation, enabling direct learning from disabled people as experts.

Previous research examining the early impact on care managers' work activity patterns of implementing the IB pilots in England (Jacobs *et al.*, 2013) found that care managers with IB holders on their caseload were spending more time assessing needs and in support planning than they did in standard care management. Care managers and other stakeholders in the SDS test sites commented on the bureaucracy surrounding implementing SDS, reporting that the paperwork involved in new assessment systems was 'time-consuming' and, in some cases, 'overwhelming', despite being broadly enthusiastic about the concept of SDS and/or personalisation. This finding is supported by the Community Care and Unison survey of social care professionals across the UK (Dunning, 2011), which found increasing numbers of social care professionals saying that personalisation was overly bureaucratic and impeding their ability to support self-assessment effectively.

Constant revisions and changes to systems in the test site local authorities led to much criticism of the new processes from care managers, who commented on low morale within social work teams, with heightened stress and high staff sickness levels as a result. Procedures felt 'cumbersome', with a typical comment from care managers being: 'it is a huge piece of additional work'. While some argued that the new systems were justified to implement SDS and represented improvement in how assessment was carried out, others stated that, unless the burden of bureaucracy for front-line workers was addressed, the desired roll out of SDS would not take place. A key contention in all of the test sites was the increased time spent on records (including completing new financial assessment forms) and inputting to computer systems designed for SDS, which were said to be taking front-line workers away from direct work with users.

Promoting SDS, raising awareness and the need for training

Implementing SDS requires local authorities to engage in a wide range of promotional and awareness-raising activities not only internally with their own staff but also with users, carers and external service providers with whom they have service contracts. In exploring the training activities in the IB pilot sites in England, Manthorpe *et al.* (2010a) conclude that the personalisation of social care requires major investment in training and skills development. Front-line staff need not only to understand the ethos and values of personalisation and SDS, but also to be skilled in delivering new systems of supported self-assessment, outcomes-focused planning and capacity-building approaches, and to be confident in supporting users to access DPs. The fundamental emphasis on users being experts in their own problems, on co-production and on an outcomes-focused approach, have major implications for the training and development of the social care workforce who are at the front-line of delivering this agenda. Ensuring the workforce is skilled in the delivery of new approaches under the umbrella of SDS is crucial to successful implementation. This has been recognised and responded to by local authorities implementing the shift to SDS in policy and practice (Kettle *et al.*, 2011; Ridley *et al.*, 2011). In South Lanarkshire as elsewhere, initial stages involved considerable investment in providing personalisation workshops and in developing an outcomes-focused approach (Kettle *et al.*, 2011). The test sites similarly engaged in extensive programmes of awareness raising and information giving about SDS as well as delivering specialist training programmes on the seven steps in the *In Control* model and person-centred planning methods. Training, along with leadership, had been identified by the Scottish Government as a key theme to be addressed by the test site investment. As SDS was rolled out across the councils, the need for training and development continued (Ridley *et al.*, 2012).

In contrast to findings from the ADASS survey (2013), which claims the social care workforce in England and Wales are 'well equipped to deliver personalisation', the survey of care managers in the Scottish test sites was less optimistic. It found that, although the majority had accessed some form of training, fewer believed they had gained the skills or knowledge to make SDS work, including how to put an outcomes-led support package together and prepare assessments and costings for IBs to be considered by RAS panels (Ridley *et al.*, 2012). This finding differed between the test sites, and there was both positive and negative experience in all the test sites. Similarly, the IBSEN study in England found implementation of training to embed personalisation in social care practice to vary greatly between local authorities (Manthorpe *et al.*, 2010a). Furthermore, while the majority across all three test sites felt their understanding of SDS had increased, this did not translate into having sufficient information and skills to support their users to access SDS, thereby suggesting an underlying need for further training and support for front-line staff. Nor was better awareness equated with positive views of SDS, as the overriding perception, especially from care managers from Glasgow, was that SDS was being used to make cuts – an issue we explore more fully in Chapter 5. As one care manager commented in the survey: 'The term SDS/personalisation is newspeak for we'll decide what reduced services you get.'

More than half of care managers in Dumfries & Galloway said they did not have enough information about SDS or did not feel skilled enough to access SDS for their users, and 56% did not feel suitably trained. A similar proportion of care managers in Highland did not feel suitably trained to deliver SDS, regardless of whether or not they had received training during the test site. Most appreciated the values embedded in SDS and personalisation and found the 'success stories', which characterised promotional events, to be positive and inspiring. However, several care managers from this area expressed concern about whether these continued to be realistic or achievable in the current climate. There was a fundamental mismatch between the aspirational nature of SDS – as alluded to by Needham's (2011b) analysis of the personalisation narrative – and the reality of what was achievable given budget cuts.

Despite a range of training programmes, therefore, the consensus of opinion among users, carers and care managers at the end of Scotland's test sites was that the training of front-line workers in new systems needed to improve if access to SDS was to expand in the future, which was later confirmed by the self-review of Scottish local authorities regarding SDS implementation (Self-directed Support

Scotland, 2013). Not feeling suitably trained to be able to access SDS for their users was related to the perception that the processes were constantly changing and being refined, and this was compounded by the challenges the care managers experienced when justifying funding for support packages. Care managers highlighted a discrepancy between the promotion of SDS to the public and how it was presented to staff. In Glasgow in particular, care managers highlighted how the council made it clear to them that they needed to make budget savings through SDS, and yet were promoting personalisation to the public as offering a better way to meet users' aspirations – a situation that they said led to false and unrealistic expectations of what was possible.

Regulation and development of the social care workforce
The issue of regulating PAs employed by users has raised concerns amid the broader climate of personalisation. In England, Leece and Leece (2011) underline the apparent contradictions of government policy, whereby the modernisation agenda has imposed increased regulation, registration and inspection on practitioners in a climate where DP users may employ their own staff with few safeguards. Any enforcement of criminal record checks (Disclosure and Barring Service, in England; Enhanced Disclosure, in Scotland) has been seen by many as undermining the principles of user-led support, thereby leaving users with only an option to undertake these type of checks. Manthorpe *et al.*, (2010b) finds that almost half of the DP users interviewed in England failed to undertake such checks for potential PA or to take up their references.

In Scotland, Disclosure Scotland clearance for PAs employed directly by users is not mandatory, and an extensive study of the PA workforce in Scotland (Reid Howie Associates, 2010) found a significant minority do not use such checks. Mixed views were expressed in this study about the benefits of registrations, with PAs generally more positive than employers. Recognised benefits included increased protection for employers, 'professionalisation' of the PA role and potentially more support and development opportunities, while the disadvantages were that it might undermine the flexibility of SDS and lead to delays and/or restrictions in recruiting PAs. Elsewhere in other cash payment systems in Europe, regulation of PAs has been found to be higher (Christensen, 2012). In Norway, for example, a more formal process of regulation has been documented throughout a number of studies.

SDS and adult support and protection in Scotland have constituted important policy initiatives for more than a decade. At the core of both is a concern with the provision of support to people who rely on services; the former focuses on the promotion of greater choice and control for users in identifying their needs and ways of meeting them, while the latter considers how adults who might be deemed as 'at risk of harm' are supported and protected. It has been argued that there are inherent tensions between these two policies in matters of empowerment and protection that are going unaddressed (Hunter *et al.*, 2012; Manthorpe *et al.*, 2010b). While not disputing the importance of providing support that increases users' choice and control, with reference to complex case studies in learning disabilities, Lymbery and Morley (2012) argue that it is equally important to act in such a way as to ensure users' safety and that of others.

Despite disparities in the extent of development because of the early momentum provided by the *In Control* project in England, the IBSEN research report (Glendinning *et al.* 2008) and the evaluation of the Scottish SDS test sites (Ridley *et al.*, 2011) similarly report that these two policies were 'twin-tracking' rather than intersecting in their implementation. The Scottish study found little awareness in SDS circles of the implications for adult support and protection concerns and increased potential for abuse of those managing their own budgets, commenting that lead officers for adult protection seemed to be 'bystanders' in the implementation of SDS with few system or practice linkages between the two strands of activity (Hunter *et al.*, 2012).

Conclusions

Experience in Scotland, as elsewhere in the UK, demonstrates that implementing personalisation implies not only radical overhaul of local authority systems of assessment, support planning and resource allocation, but also has the profound implications for the social care workforce and the role of social workers and care managers in particular. It has been recognised that a fundamental shift in the power dynamics of the support relationship is required, with the role of social work becoming more one of facilitator, involving and engaging, and that working in co-production with users implies a paradigm shift in the support relationship. Whether or not this results in social work returning to traditional core social work values and practice, or instead represents a major threat and challenge to the profession with the need for a 'new script' for public services (Leadbeater, 2004), has yet to unfold. It is clear from recent research, however, including the evaluations of the SDS test sites, that it is not proving an easy transition, made even more problematic by swingeing cuts to public finances.

Much has been written about the potential transformation of social work posed by personalisation, and the SDS test sites' and other local authorities' experience highlights key challenges for local authorities, which need to ensure the social care workforce is suitably trained and skilled to carry out new roles and approaches as expected. There are contradictory claims about the readiness of the social care workforce across the UK to make this transformation. The emphasis on the contribution that users can make to solving their own problems at either an individual or community level is a double-edged sword, particularly at a time of economic crisis, when the objective is 'not simply … to improve service quality by "bringing the user in" but also … to cut costs, by making the user do more for themselves' (Bovaird and Loeffler, 2012, p. 6).

The limited user involvement at a strategic planning level that was evident in the SDS test sites was a critical omission, and one that needs to change if a new paradigm shift in the professional–user relationship is to be fully embraced. In the context of austerity, discussion in policy and guidance documents of models of co-production based on a notable shift in power from professionals to users, which is central to earlier ideas of person-centredness, will become increasingly important for front-line workers and service planners (Scottish Government, 2014c). For many, the apparent contradictions between the heightened regulation of social care over the past decade sit uncomfortably with the lack of alignment between the twin agendas of SDS and adult protection. As Providers & Personalisation (2014) conclude, SDS requires major culture and systems change not just for providers but also for regulators of standards in social care. Furthermore, given the unique legislative position in Scotland with the Adult Support and Protection Act 2007 (ASPA), a significant culture shift in thinking on the part of professionals is required and the realisation that SDS interventions will have to be informed by ASPA.

CHAPTER 5

Personalisation in an Age of Austerity

Introduction

Discussion in this book so far has explored the origins of the personalisation agenda, through the emergence of DPs, the shift to IBs and PBs in England and, more recently, through the introduction of SDS in Scotland. This was examined initially in chapters 1 and 2 by focusing on the discourses underpinning policy development and key conceptual debates, from the disability movement, a neo-liberal push to develop care markets and wider 'modernising' influences across government and the third sector. Chapters 3 and 4 developed many of these themes by looking at empirical findings from the test site pilots for SDS in Scotland and the impact of other PB schemes across the UK.

Here we turn to look at the broader context for policy change as personalisation schemes across the UK and farther afield are implemented and sustained within a climate of acute economic uncertainty. West (2013) argues the rapid implementation of personalisation strategies has underlined an 'ideological grip' (Glynos, 2001) on its advocates and policymakers. Yet questions have been raised as to how the mantra of user choice and control can be successfully implemented within existing social care budgets (Beresford, 2013; Slasberg *et al.*, 2013; Beresford, 2009; Ferguson, 2007). Indeed, as the economic crisis of 2008 took hold and the UK government promoted a programme of austerity in an attempt to counter the impact, the role of personalisation and its potential to facilitate independent living for disabled people was called into question. Away from the UK, successive governments have also targeted support for disabled people as a key focus for public sector spending cuts. As such, there is a broad consensus within the disability community across Europe that disabled people are bearing the brunt of the austerity measures (Hauben *et al.*, 2012). This chapter looks at these issues more closely by reviewing how the austerity changes have impacted on personalisation strategies in the UK and then by examining examples in Europe.

Personalisation, direct payments and the discourse of cost-efficiency

Since implementation of the DP legislation in the late 1990s and the promotion of personalisation by Leadbeater (2008) and others (Duffy, 2010a; Department of Health, 2006), a discourse of cost-efficiency has been a key feature of policy promotion in the UK. Throughout the 1990s, successive dismissals of DP legislation on the statute were brought to an end when the British Council of Disabled People commissioned research, which, in articulating the merits of DPs, also showed them to be up to 40% cheaper than directly provided services (Zarb and Nadash, 1994). This proved a turning point in securing the support of the then Conservative government, whereby DPs were positioned as an appendage to existing plans to marketise and deregulate community care services (Pearson, 2000). While the 40% figure has never been realised in practice, in subsequent years Leadbeater (2008) and others (Needham, 2011a; 2011b; Duffy, 2010a) have also made the link between personalisation and cost-efficiency, suggesting that these strategies would lead to savings as high as 45%. Although higher spending alone is not enough to secure better outcomes for social care users, adequate resourcing of local schemes has clearly been an ongoing concern. Research has continually emphasised the importance of support frameworks as part of the policy infrastructure. More specifically, user-led and community-based support organisations, working as part of a new strategic partnership and co-producing on equal terms with commissioning authorities, have been seen as central to securing positive user outcomes (see chapters 2 and 4).

This need for resources has been underlined by Slasberg *et al.* (2012), who found that, where optimum outcomes occur for users of personalised services, better funding levels were a key factor. They and others (Slasberg *et al.*, 2012; 2013; Cabinet Office, 2005) contend that it is the *DP* element – i.e. the freedom for the individual user to choose and purchase their services – that offers the best experience and improved outcomes for the individual. Conversely, as discussed in Chapter 3, through SDS and PBs the main determinant of resources – the RAS – has proved to be a highly contentious aspect of the personalisation programme in social care (Slasberg *et al.*, 2012). As stated in Chapter 3, a survey of PB holders carried out by the London Self-directed Support Forum in 2013 reported that, in the majority of cases, the RAS seemed neither to be matching need nor coming closer to ensuring adequate financial resources. In most cases, it had in fact reduced people's budgets (Beresford, 2013). Likewise, detailed analysis by Series and Clements (2013) of how the RAS worked in twenty councils across England found it to be a poor indicator of how much support people actually required. The nexus of 'control' promoted at the heart of the personalisation strategy has often been presented as entirely positive, and that, if people simply have choice and control through PBs or SDS, the actual size of the budget is unimportant (Slasberg *et al.*, 2012). As the austerity cuts began to take hold, this assertion became ever more dubious.

For many local authorities across the UK, the timing of the economic crisis coincided with the rolling out of personalisation programmes in social care. Notably in Scotland, the 2013 Act came into force just as many of the austerity measures were beginning to take hold. This has seen overall Scottish spending reduced by about 11% in real terms across a four-year period, leaving a 7% cut in resources across local authority spending and 37% in capital spending (Scottish Government, 2012). Analysis by the Scottish Government has indicated that the worst of the cuts has yet to emerge – with the full impact of changes expected by 2016 (Scottish Government, 2014a). As suggested, this has clearly placed a significant challenge at the core principles of choice, flexibility and control. As Wood (2011) suggests, budget cuts are likely to limit personalisation schemes in two ways: by reducing an individual's eligibility for PBs (and/or SDS); and by making personalisation in its widest sense more difficult, as budgets are limited to covering only basic roles such as personal care in a home setting.

In Ridley *et al.*'s (2011) follow-up study of the SDS test sites in Scotland, concern was expressed by front-line workers over the impact of austerity measures at the same time as SDS implementation. While senior social work managers emphasised that SDS was being pursued to achieve better outcomes for users, some managers referred to how advocates of personalisation had stressed that policy could generate cost savings. Many respondents from one area in the study failed to answer survey questions relating to a link between austerity cuts and the implementation of SDS. However, in one of the test sites, the response rate was much higher, and a majority of care managers directly equated SDS as a tool to facilitate budget cuts. This perception was not helped by the introduction of a stringent financial assessment for determining user contributions to social care, which in some cases resulted in users disengaging with SDS entirely. Similarly, a clear majority of care managers felt that public expenditure cuts were having an adverse effect on policy implementation. Across each local authority, concerns were also raised by front-line staff about the gap between an 'idealistic' implementation of SDS, the promotion of independent living goals and what was actually possible in the current financial climate. These findings reiterated earlier surveys of staff working in the field. Notably, the 2011 National Community Care/Unison survey of PBs in England found that 83% of the respondent practitioners stated that cuts to adult care would impede the operation of PBs. Likewise, 33% considered resourcing to be the greatest barrier to making progress with personalisation. Clearly, no one would knowingly opt for an inferior or poor-quality product or service, yet that may be all that is available locally (Witcher, 2013).

For West (2013), the apparent contradiction between the increased freedoms associated with personalisation and the highly unsympathetic fiscal context in which the policy has emerged has been a key focus of her work. Part of her research reports on practice from an English local authority where austerity cuts of around 30% in the social care budget had been put in place. West found that, despite the cutbacks, the council went ahead with a proposed personalised scheme and presented it as part of a 'transformation strategy', which would purportedly help widen the social care market and drive out perceived inefficiencies in service provision. However, only as the programme was implemented did tightening of the eligibility criteria become apparent. This resulted in only persons assessed as having critical needs being eligible for assistance. As West shows, this restriction meant that, for many, the very possibility of even obtaining a PB was denied through newly implemented processes of resource rationalisation. While the financial difficulties are clearly acute for all local authorities, West's work highlights the way in which cohorts of social care users have been left outside new systems of personalised support, at the same time as community services have already been dismantled. In Scotland, where DPs were seen sceptically by many local authorities as a form of 'backdoor privatisation' (Pearson, 2004), concerns have also been expressed by the trade union movement over SDS and particularly the timing of implementation during a period of austerity. In Glasgow, seemingly little has occurred to allay these fears, as the rolling out of SDS coincided with an 11% cut from the £89 million social care budget during 2012/13 (Main, 2013). In explaining the cuts, the local authority has presented personalisation as a strategy for services to be delivered more efficiently.

Writing before the onset of the austerity changes, Ferguson (2007) describes the shift in baseline support through personalisation as tantamount to 'enforced individualism'. Hall (2011) focuses more specifically on the impact of the transition to more personalised services on people with learning difficulties. In doing this, he and others (see Needham, 2013) express concern over the loss of collective provision in local areas, which many users associate with a sense of belonging, safety and support. More recently, Ferguson (2012) and others (Dodd, 2013) argue that the social justice values associated with personalisation policies, which were so strongly promoted by the disability movement, have been subsumed by neo-liberalism. Therefore, rather than extend individual autonomy, Ferguson warns that policies such as SDS will be used by cash-strapped councils to make savings from their services. This is underlined by Roulstone *et al.*:

> By simply changing the language slightly from 'personalisation' to 'personalised solutions', we can undertake a policy

sleight of hand that increasingly expects self-determination and self-provisioning to prevail in an era of chronic austerity (Roulstone *et al.*, 2013, p. 2).

Austerity and disability: Challenges for a personalised vision of social care

Even before the economic crisis and the rolling out of the UK Coalition government's subsequent austerity programme, questions were already emerging over the resourcing of personalisation strategies across all user groups (see Lymbery, 2012; Beresford, 2009; Ferguson, 2007). Despite Prime Minister David Cameron's assertions that the austerity measures would 'affect every single person in the country' (Cameron, 2010), for the current generation of disabled people the impact of the cuts has been particularly acute (Wood and Grant, 2012; 2010), with reforms impacting across all areas of life (Campbell *et al.*, 2012). As a core funder of social care services, the cuts have been particularly severe for local authorities and, as shown, most departments across the UK have faced budget reductions of around 30% (West, 2013), with 81% required to limit their funding support to those with substantial or critical needs (Wood and Grant, 2012). In addition, many local authorities have been forced to close disability support services (Wood and Grant, 2012) – resources clearly identified as being essential for the effective operation of personalised support (Barnes and Mercer, 2006).

It is not simply direct cuts to local authority budgets that have transformed the funding environment for social care, but also a network of measures through which the cumulative impact will erode the daily living and support structures of those either in work and/or at home. A key example of this looks set to emerge through the proposed closure of the ILF in 2015 in England and Wales and the transference of existing payments to local authorities. The ILF is a registered charity funded through the Department for Work and Pensions with payments facilitated through local authorities. Since its inception in 1988 (and through its subsequent incarnations), it has paid additional cash sums, which have formed integral parts of support packages for disabled people with the highest needs. For the estimated 21,000 users, the ILF has been central to facilitating independent living, allowing users to work, go to university or even just leave the house. Indeed, these types of positive experiences formed an integral part of the campaign for DPs (see Kestenbaum, 1992). The shift of payment responsibility to local authorities has been widely criticised by disabled people and their organisations (Campbell, 2014), as questions are raised as to how already cash-strapped authorities will cover ILF costs without ring-fenced payments in place. With social care provision already at very low levels, and examples emerging where councils are tightening their eligibility criteria so that they fund persons only with 'substantial' or 'critical' needs, it is difficult to see how this additional cohort of spending will be contained (White, 2013).

As well as the cuts to local authority budgets, broader changes to the social security system have also directly affected the day-to-day choices and freedoms of many social care users. Under the austerity programme, payments funded through the social security system have also been targeted. This has included a tightening of eligibility for new Housing Benefit claimants – a change impacting disproportionately on disabled people seeking entry to lower paid work – and the introduction of a 'bedroom tax', where benefit will be lost to those in local authority or housing association properties deemed to have an extra bedroom. (Changes announced in May 2014 will allow the Scottish Government to transfer the power to set the cap on discretionary housing payments to help people on housing benefit who need extra help. In effect, this decision resulted in the end of bedroom tax in Scotland, although no additional resources were made available for this [Watt, 2014].)

Meanwhile, the abolition of non-means tested Disability Living Allowance (DLA) – implemented in 1992 to help disabled people cope with the extra costs of disability – in favour of the medically assessed Personal Independence Payment (PIP) is already proving detrimental to the daily support structures of those either in work and/or at home. Estimates suggest that around 600,000 people will have entitlement to DLA removed, many of whom will lose the qualifying award to receive a car through the Motability Scheme (Samuel, 2012). Therefore, the reconfiguration of these funds – either through a shift to a more rigid medicalised regime via PIP or by their removal (ILF) and the overall reduction of local authority funding – will sharply erode the scope for independent living for many disabled people and will require cash-strapped local authorities to pick up the shortfall. Since October 2010 – a few months after the announcement of the Coalition's emergency budget – the think-tank Demos, in a longitudinal piece of research, has highlighted the negative effects that the series of welfare reforms have had on disabled people (see Wood and Grant, 2012; 2010; Wood *et al.*, 2012; Wood, 2011). It estimates that 3.6 million disability benefit claimants in the UK will lose £9 billion in benefit income by 2015.

Austerity and the challenges to personalisation programmes across Europe

As the austerity programme has unfolded in the UK, evidence from Europe shows a similar pattern of cuts to securing the long-term personalised support for disabled people. Indeed to date, the cumulative effects of these changes led the European Agency for Fundamental Rights to warn, in March 2012, that the economic crisis would progressively erode the advances that have been made in establishing and promoting the rights of disabled people (Hauben *et al.*, 2012). The following section explores how these cuts have been rolled out across key European countries. Clearly, the empirical base for exploring these changes is emerging rapidly, and at the time of writing one of the most helpful overviews was available through Hauben *et al.*'s (2012) study, which sets out to examine the evidence at European and national level as to the effects of the economic crisis on the rights and status of disabled people.

The austerity era has also coincided with increased social media activity by individuals and groups of disabled people (Trevisan, 2013). For example, the European Network on Independent Living (ENIL) (www.enil.eu; accessed 11 August 2014), Disabled People Against the Cuts (DPAC) (on Twitter: DPAC@Dis_PPL_Protest) and the postings on *Diary of a Benefit Scrounger* (http://diaryofabenefitscrounger. blogspot.co.uk; accessed 11 August 2014) have all regularly used various forms of social media such as Facebook and Twitter to document the ongoing impact of policy changes in the UK and farther afield. As will be shown, Hauben *et al.* (2012) and others highlight the widespread reduction and/or abandonment of cash-based, personalised support schemes for disabled people across Europe. Discussion here will draw on some of the key themes emanating from the austerity cuts across different European welfare regimes. While the extent of the cuts and their impact on disabled people differ, it is clear that advances in independent living through personalised support have been widely compromised by the drive to cut costs.

Mapping the pattern of austerity and personalisation across Europe

Hauben *et al.*'s (2012) review reveal that the impact of the economic crisis on the social care sector substantially differs between member state countries. Countries such as Germany, Austria and those in Scandinavia appeared to be facing fewer reductions in social benefits and social services, particularly in contrast to Greece, Ireland, Spain and Portugal. Others such as Hungary and the UK have tended to focus their austerity measures through reform of social security systems (Hauben *et al.*, 2012; Heise and Lierse, 2011) with the focus of the austerity approach framed at least in part through a discourse of modernisation and reform of the role of state support for disabled people. However, the overall pattern indicates that the austerity measures in member states have impacted on social security and healthcare spending to a lesser extent *or* with more diversity among the member states (see Karanikolas *et al.*, 2013). Conversely, social services appear to be the hardest hit and have thereby impacted on disabled people disproportionately.

Discussion of the austerity cuts in the UK has shown that there is evidence to suggest that access to a personalised budget – paid either through social insurance-based schemes, non-contributory-based schemes or, more typically, through social assistance or social care support – has become increasingly restricted as the austerity cuts have taken hold. This is a trend that is clearly being replicated across Europe. Even in member states that have well-established, independent living schemes, changes to eligibility criteria have become apparent. Notably in Sweden – whereby PA has been established as a right since 1994 and which has often been hailed as being most consistent in how the disability movement and organisations of disabled people want PA organised (see, for example, Oliver and Barnes, 1998) – access to support has been eroded. This has seen about 5% of Swedish PA users now losing their PAs after their needs have been reviewed (ENIL, 2013). Prior to the crisis, the Swedish scheme was available to anyone assessed as needing up to twenty hours per week. PA was then made available to support any area of day-to-day living where it was required. However, changes from the organising Social Insurance Agency in Sweden have now instigated a re-categorisation of the eligibility rules, through introduction of the term 'active time'. This means that, if someone has a need for assistance for a few minutes now and then but manages in between, they are only granted support for the 'active time'.

Elsewhere in Scandinavia, legislation has been developed under the auspices of 'personal assistance' but in terms that look set to undermine the social freedoms and independence of its potential users. In Norway, a Bill was presented to Parliament in spring 2013, which offered entitlement to user-led personal assistance. However, Bolling (2013) argues that the proposed legislation is so weak that it risks offering disabled people in Norway poorer services than they currently receive. Under the guidelines set out, the Bill would limit people leaving their municipality with the support of their PA. As such, any personal assistance package would be based solely on social care in a home setting. Another way of reducing access to support has been apparent through the use of waiting lists. In Ireland, waiting lists for social and healthcare have sharply increased and more than 25% of persons with physical or sensory impairment are on waiting lists for access to an assessment service or for PA and support services (Hauben *et al.*, 2012). Likewise in Belgium's Flemish community, the PA waiting list for personal assistance has increased to 50,000 people – resulting in an estimated five- to ten-year wait for this type of support (Ratza, 2012).

Changing directions?

The pace of change through which governments across Europe have developed austerity plans in reaction to the economic crisis has inevitably provoked criticism and – in some cases – a change in direction as their likely impact becomes apparent. In January 2011, the Dutch government in its Persoorsgebouden Budget decided to decrease its PB scheme drastically, from the beginning of the following year. Under these plans, new users assessed as being in need of non-residential care support would no longer qualify for a PB. This would have seen 90% of users losing their PB by 2014 (DAA News, 2011). However, the budget pact secured by parties in the Kundiz coalition in late 2012 put forward funds of €150 million to reverse these cuts (Hauben *et al.*, 2012).

In the UK, plans announced in the Coalition Government's emergency budget in June 2010 set out to remove the mobility component of DLA for those living in residential care. However, the decision was subsequently revoked in response to extensive lobbying from disability groups (Owen, 2013). In November 2013, the Court of Appeal ruled that the government's decision to shut the ILF in 2015 failed to assess the impact of the closure on the lives of recipients and was therefore in breach of the public sector Equality Duty. The five disabled people making the challenge argued that removal of the payments would dramatically compromise their independence by forcing them to give up work and/or move into residential care (Butler, 2013). The decision to close the fund was upheld in March 2014 even though, by the UK government's own impact assessment, it was stated that it would have 'adverse effects' on disabled people (Campbell, 2014). The future of the ILF was complicated further in April 2014, when the Scottish Government announced a £5.5 million investment to re-open the fund and continue with existing payments (Scottish Government, 2014b). The budget will be made up from a transfer of current funding alongside the additional new monies and will be run by a new third sector organisation, with the input of disabled people. This means that, from July 2015, a new Scottish ILF will run across Scotland, while elsewhere in the UK the ILF will close.

Elsewhere in Europe, mobility allowances have been cut. In Greece, there are no PB schemes as such, but financial support services, which enable disabled people to live more independently, have been cancelled. This has included the removal of transport allowances, which allow disabled people to visit assessment centres (Hauben *et al.*, 2012). Austerity cuts have also prompted some EU member states to put on hold plans to develop PB schemes. Notably in Portugal, the introduction of PBs for disabled people was due to be implemented in 2011, but has been delayed indefinitely (Hauben *et al.*, 2012). In Spain, higher co-payment fees and stricter eligibility criteria to the Autonomy and Care of Dependency schemes have been put in place, despite ongoing increased demand from users and their families (Hauben *et al.*, 2012).

Other types of personalised support have been reduced, provoking concerns over the implications for social inclusion. Notably, the Council of Europe has warned that Spain's austerity programme was having a serious impact on many disabled children who had been left in mainstream schools without any personalised support (BBC News, 2013). In France, the 2005 Equality Act was welcomed at least in part for its shift towards a social model framework for tackling disability issues (Calvez, 2010). However, this has since been undermined by delays in the programme to make all public buildings accessible by 2015. By 2012, only around 15% had met the required standards – a figure directly correlated with the economic costs of doing so (Willsher, 2012).

Conclusions

It is clear from the discussion outlined in this chapter that personalisation programmes across the UK and in the rest of Europe are being hit disproportionately hard by austerity measures. This has had implications not only for long-standing PA schemes such as in Sweden, the Netherlands, Belgium and parts of the UK, but also in countries such as Portugal and Greece where personalisation has yet to be fully developed. Throughout the 1990s and up until the time of the financial crisis in 2008, changes in legislation and service provision across Europe emerged to promote and safeguard the rights and independent living choices of disabled people. However, the onset of austerity measures and specific targeting of social care users look set to undermine these changes severely. More broadly, as Hauben *et al.* (2012) argue, a major consequence of these shifts is that progress on the rights of disabled people as laid out in the UN CRPD is now in jeopardy. In light of these concerns, the European Agency for Fundamental Rights issued a statement in March

2012 referring to reports of the 'extremely negative effects' of the austerity measures on disabled people, despite reassurances from European institutions that they would be safeguarded.

The next and final chapter will synthesise the evidence presented throughout the book and assess possible ways forward for the personalisation agenda as Scotland moves to embrace a new era in social care provision with implementation of the 2013 Act. As successive governments have been keen to embrace change, we now ask how this can be achieved in light of the acute economic pressures and wider issues relating to values underpinning the vision for SDS.

CHAPTER 6

Discussion and Conclusions: Self-directed Support and the Future of Personalised Social Care in Scotland

Introduction

As local authorities in Scotland operationalise the new legislation for SDS, it is clear that April 2014 will signify a major watershed and a cultural and system change for social care. However, as we have stated throughout this book, the economic climate for social care funding, fundamental problems with the RAS and the wider welfare reforms as they impinge on disabled people remain hostile to promoting the founding principles of personalisation – as developed by the independent living movement and that put people at the centre of decision-making about their lives. It is clear that, for some commentators, the early alignment of DPs and personalisation as a means to achieve possible cost savings in social care has left an unhelpful legacy and, as discussion showed in Chapter 5, this has rendered the timing of the 2014 implementation drive to promote SDS to be particularly problematic. Clearly, this is not simply a problem for Scotland. The previous chapter established how the vision for personalised social care in countries across Europe – from those with more entrenched 'rights-based' systems such as Sweden to those in the initial stages of planning such as Portugal and Greece – has also been compromised.

This chapter revisits the key themes discussed throughout the book. In particular, we build on the notion of SDS as an 'evolving concept' set out in Chapter 3 and the changing cultures of care through the integration of co-production strategies, as detailed in

Chapter 2. While acknowledging the challenges of the economic backdrop for implementation, we highlight a number of localised initiatives which have embraced co-production as the basis of social care systems. Indeed, given the wealth of discussion emerging around personalisation and attempts from within the disability movement by long-term advocates of person-centred support (see, for example, Beresford, 2014a; 2014b; 2013; Roulstone *et al.*, 2013; Zarb, 2013; Joseph Rowntree Foundation, 2011) to reposition the current agenda, there clearly remains enthusiasm to achieve a more positive outcome within these new systems of care. As the following section outlines, evidence of where SDS and personalisation is likely to have the most positive outcome for users requires a refocusing on the principles of person-centred support and co-production, which lie at the heart of policy. In looking at this in more detail, we examine examples of good practice emerging in Scotland and England, and set out themes for moving the personalisation agenda forward positively, as proposed by one of the leading commentators in this field.

Reinvigorating user roles: Innovation and co-production in a time of austerity

Despite the wealth of criticism of personalisation strategies, Beresford (2014b) argues that social care has many innovative grassroots developments to offer. He identifies an 'expression of a will for something different – a true evocation of personalisation or "person-centred" support' (Beresford, 2014b). Initiatives such as those led by the Standards We Expect consortium (Joseph Rowntree Foundation, 2011) have set out their vision for person-centred support and developing 'bottom-up' ways of challenging barriers within local areas in England. While they have emphasised the acute crisis of funding in social care and difficulties in achieving personalised outcomes in a hostile economic climate, they also argue that the funding shortfall is intrinsically linked to the continued existence of a social care culture that remains at odds with person-centred support and the principle of self-determination. Clearly, there are important differences in the principles and practices of social care north and south of the border. These may be further accentuated after the 2014 referendum vote, making cross-border comparisons ever more difficult

(Kettle *et al.*, 2011). However, to date the experiences of personalisation in England do raise some important issues that clearly resonate with the experiences of those who have been working to implement SDS in Scotland, and from which reformers north and south of the border can learn. These are outlined in the following sections.

One of the major voices in the Standards We Expect consortium is Peter Beresford. Although highly critical of the current personalisation drive in England, Beresford (2014b) highlights examples of innovative practice and advances an agenda for change. In doing this, he has promoted a series of local initiatives developed in Hampshire – one of the first areas in the UK to adopt indirect payment schemes in the 1980s. This has involved establishing a clear framework for co-production – by pooling DPs and involving users and local providers in service commissioning. In 2013, Hampshire County Council and Spectrum (the disabled people's organisation) jointly organised a competition to develop innovative approaches to home care. Each of the local user-led groups taking part in the competition received some funding support, independent guidance and expertise to help them with their bid. Proposals included a smart technology link to people's homes to provide virtual visits, non-intrusive advice and support – and, where needed, home visits and a person-centred scheme prioritising user involvement and enhanced choice of carers.

The proposals were judged by a mixed team of disabled people, users and staff from Hampshire social services. The eventual winners included: a web-based service run by disabled people to help people find reliable PAs and support staff who closely match their unique needs and preferences; and the development of a network of over fifty year olds to provide home help to support older people in maintaining their independence and well-being. The latter offered employment opportunities to older people, as well as all kinds of practical support. Both winners received £4,000 each to take their ideas forward and roll them out.

As Beresford (2014b) shows, the Hampshire initiatives demonstrated that, if a partnership between service professionals and local users can be made, then there is scope to develop personalised service options. In many ways, these types of partnership have replicated the 'unlikely marriage' between local authorities and the disability movement (Pearson, 2000), which were so key in advancing the goals of the independent living movement and securing legislation for DPs in the 1990s.

In Scotland, examples of positive practice in SDS are also emerging. Research funded by Glasgow Disability Alliance – *My Choices: A Vision for Self-directed Support* (Witcher, 2014) – was set up by a user-led organisation to explore options for disabled people to enable increased choice and control in their day-to-day lives. The project focused on the core requirements of facilitating individual choice and independent living. Like the examples in Hampshire, the Glasgow project has focused strongly on the notion of peer support and user-centred planning.

As detailed throughout this book, the availability of user-led support has been central to the successful implementation of DPs and other cash-based models of personalised support (Barnes and Mercer, 2006), but, thus far, user-led support has not been central in the development of SDS practice development. The lack of input from user-led support organisations in the strategic planning of the SDS test sites was a critical omission. Likewise in chapters 2 and 3, a more proactive role for independent advocacy in the self-assessment process has been highlighted, to ensure those with higher support needs are not excluded and to enable the rhetoric of supported self-assessment to become meaningful. One of the clear successes of the *My Choices* project was that a high level of peer support was built into its delivery. This included designated events, group meetings, group work and, where appropriate, pooled budgets. In each example, users worked together and supported each other in achieving individual goals. As Witcher emphasises, the importance of this cannot be overstated:

> It would be possible to sustain an argument that social isolation is so destructive and that it is relationships of all kinds that form the bedrock of people's lives (Witcher, 2014, p. 5).

In Chapter 5, we argued that the loss of collective services used by many disabled people is one of the worrying outcomes of the current austerity cuts (Hall, 2011) and has led to what Ferguson (2007) terms 'enforced individualism'. While the focus on individual choice is important, Witcher (2013) underlines broader concerns over a system of social care which may increase isolation and loneliness for many, as spending priorities are realigned away from community-based services. Adequate resourcing of SDS is likely to be a dominant theme in the early years of policy implementation and, as we have set out, the concerns over how financial support for disabled people is managed is a very real one. However, as the *My Choices* project found, there was no obvious or consistent relationship between the amount of money that was spent on realising individual choices and the scale of its impact (Witcher, 2014). For example, some packages involved considerable investment for a British Sign Language interpreter to be available, whereas others required only a few hundred pounds for transport costs so that the individual could attend classes of their choice. A similar finding emerged from evaluation of the SDS test sites, which found no correlation between the size of the support package and the impact of SDS on individuals' and families' lives (Ridley *et al.*, 2011). For Witcher (2014), the driving force in the success of SDS was that the support was truly person-centred and linked to self-defined outcomes.

While disability activism proved a central force in securing legislation for DPs, commentators such as Cooper (2004) suggest that there has been depoliticisation of more traditional political affiliations. Yet the era of social media has brought with it new opportunities for participation and a voice for users. In Chapter 5, this was discussed in relation to the austerity cuts and the role that disabled people's organisations such as DPAC has taken in voicing opposition to welfare reform. Dialogue between users, planners and service professionals involved in SDS will be central to successful implementation. Indeed, leading Scottish disability organisations such as Lothian Centre for Inclusive Living have set up an online campaign #makesdswork (available at URL: www.lothiancil.org.uk/get-involved-with-lothian-cil/makesdswork; accessed 11 August 2014) to encourage users to post their experiences of SDS. Other online initiatives have also been developed specifically to offer pathways to SDS for seldom-heard groups. A key example of this has come through the work of the Pilotlight project co-ordinated by the Institute for Research and Insti-tute for Research and Innovation in Social Services (IRISS, 2014). Their work has centred on a co-design approach, working in partnership with people who use and deliver services across Scotland to develop service pathways that address thorny issues encountered with SDS implementation. To date, this has involved work in two local authorities. Firstly in Moray, work has been carried out with users and professionals to promote SDS for persons with mental health problems. This resulted in the production of an online animation that explains how SDS works (see http://pilotlight.iriss.org.uk; accessed 11 August 2014). Secondly, in the Scottish Borders, a co-production team was set up to consider issues of risk and capacity, focusing on the interface of adult protection and SDS.

Routes forward for the personalisation of care

In his appraisal of the English system of personalisation, Beresford (2014a) argues that PBs can work but only if government is honest about the lack of resources available and local authorities set out their visions and values. In chapters 3 and 5, we showed how the RAS – the means of determining individual need through SDS and PBs – has already proved controversial in its implementation. As stated in Chapter 3, many commentators have been scathing in their attacks on it and even its originator, Simon Duffy, has made a formal apology for it (Duffy, 2012). For Beresford (2014a), the current practice of distorting assessments to ensure that a person's 'needs' are interpreted to fit available resources must be replaced by full transparency. He therefore sets out three underlying themes for good practice.

Firstly, he argues that social service departments must be open about the level of available resources and admit that this is important to achieving better outcomes. Clearly, adequate resourcing is a central part of attaining positive outcomes for SDS, and this has been highlighted in earlier research in England (Slasberg et al., 2013). However, as has been shown, user experiences of increased autonomy and control are not always correlated with the most expensive packages (Witcher, 2014; Ridley et al., 2011). Furthermore, the experience of Dumfries & Galloway's SDS test site shows how an 'upfront' allocation of resources early on in the process can be counterproductive if this results in a focus on entitlement to the indicative budget rather than engaging individuals, families and communities in the generation of creative, and possibly less expensive, solutions. There are, of course, dangers in promoting such an approach, and this goes back to the origins of the concept of co-production and personalisation as ways of achieving cost-effectiveness. As discussion in Chapter 4 also highlighted, the austerity cuts force an inevitable power shift in the co-production process from user to professional that is counter to the ethos of personalisation and SDS. Therefore, where there is a funding gap, this must be discussed openly with users.

Secondly, Beresford (2014a) points out that experience shows that the only real freedoms to be achieved via personalisation are through the user-led DP model. For Scotland, this may prove to be a particularly difficult issue to reconcile. DPs were never uniformly well received (see Pearson, 2004) and research findings cited in Chapter 3 showed that the majority of SDS packages and PBs were managed by local authorities. DPs may not be welcomed by all users, but unless there is a cultural shift in social care – which would see the DP option promoted more routinely – a predominance of local authority-managed SDS packages may leave many users unaware of any tangible changes to their support and, ultimately, they may feel unmoved by the SDS process. Similarly, issues around supported self-assessment need to be explored more thoroughly. Again, findings from the pilot sites in Chapter 3 indicated that this remains a highly problematic area, with the vast majority of assessments being carried out by professionals with reference to the views of relatives, rather than users themselves.

Thirdly, Beresford (2014a) turns his attention to the type of local 'care markets' being promoted through personalisation. Although the marketisation of social care is arguably at a more advanced stage in England, Scotland still has lessons to learn. Beresford argues that commissioning authorities must ensure that the price paid in the 'care market' for services is enough to provide a personalised approach. In doing this, he emphasises the need for local areas to develop a network of providers who are able to deliver flexible and responsive services and not simply block contracts with economies of scale that render personalisation irrelevant.

This should be complemented by an increased number of user-led organisations and equal access to advocacy. None of these demands is new, but they often remain ignored and/or squeezed by budget constraints despite being continually shown as being central to providing innovative and well-received services (Joseph Rowntree Foundation, 2011).

Beresford's (2014a) themes for good practice outlined above link in well with the three levels of personalisation – prevention, participation and consumer choice – as set out in the *Changing Lives* review (Scottish Executive, 2006). If these are to be realised, it will be important to integrate these issues into practice from the onset of policy implementation.

For Morris (2014), one of the fundamental problems for users of personalised care remains the fragmentation of services and budgets. Although attempts have been made to develop a more integrated structure, the earlier experiences of the 2008 IB pilots in England failed to bring together the six core funding streams because of a lack of understanding of the policy rationale and a failure by the key government departments to work together. More recently, plans to integrate services have been subjected to ongoing delay and confusion. Notably, the Department of Health's Better Care fund – an initiative developed to bring together health and social care services by investing in joint funding of community-based services – was delayed due to concern over cost savings from ministers (Parker, 2014). By contrast, the Public Bodies (Joint Working) (Scotland) Act 2014 puts in place a framework for integrating health and social care in Scotland. Although this covers only the merging of two funding streams, it sets in place a new culture of collaborative working, which has the potential gradually to break down some of the barriers to independent living.

Concluding comments

As Scotland enters a new era for social care, much remains unknown about how SDS will operate as a mainstream policy framework. The magnitude of transformational change inherent in implementing such a major policy as SDS, both to local authority systems and to support roles, and which is demonstrated by the experiences documented in this book, should not be underestimated. While self-directed support may on one level appear a simple idea, the experiences from pilots across the UK, including the SDS test sites, demonstrate that, to be implemented in a meaningful way, SDS demands a major paradigm shift in the relationship between users and professionals. Of course, this is not new, and has been lobbied for by the disability movement for many years. As Chapter 3 highlighted, the switch to a national rollout of SDS in Scotland (and elsewhere in the UK) was made on the basis of very limited research from a series of only small pilot projects. Hence there is a need for a much wider evidence base to examine a range of implementation issues. Likewise, the type of innovative practice permitted through the additional resourcing allocated for the test site projects may prove critical in securing successful outcomes in the new era of SDS. The differential approaches to SDS across Scotland may ultimately reflect an attempt to develop social care in line with locality issues and the potential to embrace a more communitarian understanding of co-production (see Chapter 2). However, the current picture presents a very uneven postcode lottery.

Recognition of the uncertainty in new roles for social work and other front-line staff – as described in Chapter 4 – must be reflected in substantive training and development programmes across local authorities. Whether or not new roles are in line with the core values and philosophy of social work, or whether they represent a radical departure from traditional social work and a new paradigm, has yet to be determined. Experience to date suggests that the 'transformational' shift in power relationships is proving to be a challenge. Partnership with local user-led organisations will also be critical to enabling support and advocacy for users. All of this inevitably requires adequate resourcing and, with the worst of the cuts yet to emerge (Scottish Government, 2014a), it is difficult to envisage an entirely positive outcome. As this chapter has shown, there is a will to promote user-centred practice and to embrace an agenda for change, but this cannot be progressed in isolation from the austerity drive.

REFERENCES

ADASS (2009) *Personalisation and the Law: Implementing Putting People First in the Current Legal Framework*, London: Association of Directors of Adult Social Services

ADASS (2011) *ADASS Report on Personalisation Survey*, Association of Directors of Adult Social Services. Available at URL: www.adass.org.uk/uploadedFiles/adass_content/publications/policy_documents/key_documents/ADASS%20 report%20personalisation%20survey%205.pdf (accessed 2 September 2014)

ADASS (2013) *ADASS Survey Shows Personalised Social Services Being Offered to More and More Users*, London: Association of Directors of Adult Social Services press release 10 September

ADSW (2009), *Personalisation: Principles, Challenges and a New Approach*, Glasgow: OLM Publishing

Arksey, H. and Kemp, P. A. (2008) *Dimensions of Choice: A Narrative Review of Cash-for-care Schemes*, York: University of York, Social Policy Research Unit

Armstrong, F. and Alsop, A. (2010) 'Debate: Co-production can contribute to research impact in the social sciences', *Public Money & Management*, Vol. 30, No. 4, pp. 208–10; doi: 10.1080/09540962.2010.492178

Bamber, C. and Flanagan, P. (2008) 'Mental health and self-directed support', *Mental Health Today*, July/August, pp. 26–8

Barnes, C. and Mercer, G. (2006) *Independent Futures: Creating User-led Disability Services in a Disabling Society*, Bristol: Policy Press

BBC News (2013) 'Watchdog warns Spain of impact of cuts on children'. Available from URL: www.bbc.co.uk/news/world-europe-24457562 (accessed 9 January 2013)

Beresford, P. (2009) *Whose Personalisation?*, Think Pieces No. 47 (March), London: Compass

Beresford, P. (ed.) (2013) *Personalisation*, Bristol: Policy Press; available as e-book

Beresford, P. (2014a) 'Personal budgets: How the government can learn from its past mistakes', *The Guardian*, 26 February. Available from URL: www.theguardian.com/public-leaders-network/2014/feb/26/social-care-failures-personal-budgets (accessed 5 March 2014)

Beresford, P. (2014b) 'Hampshire competition paves the way for innovative approaches to home care', *The Guardian*, 19 February. Available from URL: www.theguardian.com/social-care-network/2014/feb/19/user-led-innovative-approaches-to-home-care (accessed 26 March 2014)

Bolling, J. (2013) 'Cuts and harsher conditions for disabled people in Norway'. Available from URL: www.enil.eu/news/cuts-and-harsher-conditions-for-the-disabled-in-norway (accessed 16 January 2014)

Bovaird, T. and Loeffler, E. (2012) 'From engagement to co-production: the contribution of users and communities to outcomes and public value', *Voluntas* (2012), Vol. 23, pp. 1119–38; doi 10.1007/s11266–012–9309–6

Boxall, K., Dowson, S. and Beresford, P. (2009) 'Selling individual budgets, choice and control: local and global influences on UK social care policy for people with learning difficulties', *Policy & Politics*, Vol. 37, No. 4, pp. 499–515; doi: 10.1332/030557309X445609

Butler, P. (2013) 'Five disabled people win independent living fund appeal', *The Guardian*, 6 November. Available at URL: www.theguardian.com/society/2013/nov/06/disabled-people-win-living-fund-appeal (accessed 4 August 2014)

Cabinet Office (2005) *Improving the Life Chances of Disabled People*, London: Cabinet Office

Calvez, M. (2010) *The 2005 Disability Policy in France: An Opportunity for the Development of Disability Studies*. Available at URL: http://hal.archives-ouvertes.fr/docs/00/53/58/90/PDF/EUPHA_EHESP_Calvez.pdf (accessed 28 January 2014)

Cameron, D. (2010) *The Age of Austerity*. Available at URL: www.conservatives.com/News/Speeches/2009/04/The_age_of_austerity_speech_to_the_2009_Spring_Forum.aspx (accessed 4 December 2012)

Campbell, J. (2014) 'Without the Independent Living Fund, it's a bad time to be disabled', *The Guardian*, 31 March. Available at URL: www.theguardian.com/commentisfree/2014/mar/31/independent living-fund-disabled (accessed 2 April 2014)

Campbell, J. and Oliver, M. (1996) *Disability Politics: Understanding our Past, Changing our Future*, London: Routledge

Campbell, S. J., Marsh, S., Franklin, K., Gaffney, D., Dixon, M., Leigh, J., Barnett-Cormack, S., Fon-James, R., Willis, D. *et al.* (2012) *Responsible Reform: A Report on the Proposed Changes to Disability Living Allowance*. Available at www.ekklesia.co.uk/files/response_to_proposed_dla_reforms.pdf (accessed 31 March 2014)

Carr, S. (2010) *Rough Guide to Personalisation*, London: Social Care Institute for Excellence

Carr, S. (2011) 'Enabling risk and ensuring safety: Self-directed support and personal budgets', *Journal of Adult Protection*, Vol. 13. No. 3, pp. 122–36; doi: 10.1108/14668201111160723

Carr, S. (2013) 'Personalisation, participation and policy constitution: A critique of influences and understandings', in Beresford, P. (ed) (2013) *Personalisation*, Bristol: Policy Press; available as e-book

Christensen, K. (2012) 'Towards sustainable hybrid relationships in cash-for-care systems', *Disability & Society*, Vol. 27, No. 3, pp. 399–412

Community Care and Unison (2011) *Personalisation Survey*. Available at URL: www.thinklocalactpersonal.org.uk/News/PersonalisationNewsItem/?cid=8966 (accessed 4 August 2014)

Cook, A., and Miller, E. (2012) *Talking Points. Personal Outcomes Approach. Practical Guide*, Edinburgh: Joint Improvement Team

Cooper, D. (2004) *Challenging Diversity: Rethinking Equality and the Value of Difference*, Cambridge: Cambridge University Press

Cunningham, I., and Nickson, D. (2011) *Personalisation and Its Implications for Work and Employment in the Voluntary Sector*, Glasgow: Scottish Centre for Employment Research, Strathclyde Business School and Voluntary Sector Social Services Workforce Unit

DAA News Network (2011) *The Netherlands: Personal Budgets Decimated by Cuts*. Available from URL: www.daa.org.uk/index.php?page=left-daa-news-network&daa_cat=123 (accessed 31 March 2014)

Davidson, J., Baxter, K., Glendinning, C., Jones, K., Forder, J., Caiels, J., Welch, E., Windle, K, Dolan, P. and King, D. (2012) *Personal Health Budgets: Experiences and Outcomes for Budget Holders at Nine Months. Fifth Interim Report*, London: Department of Health

Department of Health (2006) *Our Health, Our Care, Our Say: A New Direction for Community Services*, London: Department of Health

Department of Health (2007) *Putting People First: A Shared Vision and Commitment to the Transformation of Adult Social Care*, London: Department of Health

Department of Health (2008) *Transforming Social Care*, Local Authority Circular LAC (DH) 1, London: Department of Health

Department of Health (2010) *Independent Inquiry into the Care Provided by Mid-Staffordshire Health Care Trust (Francis Report)*, London: Department of Health

Dodd, S. (2013) 'Personalisation, individualism and the politics of disablement', *Disability & Society*, Vol. 28, No. 2, pp. 260–73; doi: 10.1080/09687599.2012.699283

Donnison, D. (2009) *Speaking to Power: Advocacy for Health and Social Care*, Bristol: Policy Press

Dowson, S. and Greig, R. (2009) 'The emergence of the independent support broker role', *Journal of Integrated Care*, Vol. 17, No. 4, pp. 22–30; doi: 10.1108/14769018200900028

Duffy, S. (2007) 'Care management and self-directed support', *Journal of Integrated Care*, Vol. 15, No. 5, pp. 3–14; doi: 10.1108/14769018200700033

Duffy, S. (2010a), *Future of Personalisation*, Sheffield: Centre for Welfare Reform

Duffy, S. (2010b) 'The citizenship theory of social justice: Exploring the meaning of personalisation for social workers', *Journal of Social Work Practice*, Vol. 24, No. 3, pp. 253–67; doi: 10.1080/02650533.2010.500118

Duffy, S. (2012) *An Apology*. Available at URL: www.centreforwelfarereform.org/library/by-date/an-apology.html (accessed 3 April 2014)

Dunning, J. (2010) 'Personalisation in Scotland', *Community Care*. Available at URL: www.communitycare.co.uk/2010/03/15/personalisation-in-scotland (accessed 3 April 2014)

Dunning, J. (2011) 'How bureaucracy is derailing personalisation', *Community Care*. Available at URL: www.communitycare.co.uk/2011/05/24/how-bureaucracy-is-derailing-personalisation (accessed 3 April 2014)

Edge, J. (2001) *Who's in Control? Decision-making by People with Learning Difficulties Who Have High Support Needs*, London: Values into Action

Ellis, K. (2007) 'Direct payments and social work practice: The significance of "street-level bureaucracy" in determining eligibility', *British Journal of Social*

Work, Vol. 37, pp. 405–22; doi: 10.1093/bjsw/bcm013

ENIL (2013) *Update on Personal Assistance in Sweden*. Available at URL: www.enil.eu/news/update-on-personal-assistance-in-sweden (accessed 3 April 2014)

Etherington, K., Hatton, C. and Waters, J. (2009) *Way Ahead. Our Early Experience in North Lanarkshire of Demonstrating the Impact of the In Control Approach*, Edinburgh: *In Control* Scotland

Evans, C. (2012) 'Increasing opportunities for co-production and personalisation through social work student placements in disabled people's organisations', *Social Work Education*, Vol. 31, No. 2, pp. 235–40; doi: 10.1080/02615479.2012.644969

Ferguson, I. (2007) 'Increasing user choice or privatizing risk?: The antinomies of personalisation', *British Journal of Social Work*, Vol. 37, No. 3, pp. 387–403; doi: 10.1093/bjsw/bcm016

Ferguson, I. (2012) 'Personalisation, social justice and social work: A reply to Simon Duffy', *Journal of Social Work Practice*, Vol. 26, No. 1, pp. 55–73; doi: 10.1080/02650533.2011.623771

Flynn, M. (2012) *Winterbourne View Hospital: A Serious Case Review*, Bristol: South Gloucestershire Council, South Gloucestershire Safeguarding Adults Board

Foster, M., Harris, J., Jackson, K., Morgan, H. and Glendinning, C. (2006) 'Personalised social care for adults with disabilities: A problematic concept for frontline practice', *Health and Social Care in the Community*, Vol. 14, No. 2, pp. 125–33

Gardner, A. (2011) *Personalisation in Social Work*, London: Sage Publications Learning Matters

Gershon, P. (2004) *Releasing Resources to the Front Line: Independent Review of Public Sector Efficiency*, London, HMSO

Glasby, J. and Duffy, S. (2007) *Our Health, Our Care, Our Say – What Could the NHS Learn from Individual Budgets and Direct Payments?*, Birmingham, Health Services Management Centre, University of Birmingham and *In Control*

Glasby, J. and Littlechild, R. (2009) *Direct Payments and Personal Budgets: Putting Personalisation into Practice*, 2nd edn, Bristol: Policy Press

Glendinning, C. (1992) 'Residualism versus rights: Social policy and disabled people', in Manning, N. and Page, R. (eds) (1992) *Social Policy Review 4*, Canterbury: Social Policy Association

Glendinning, C., Challis, D., Fernandez. J., Jacobs, S., Jones, K., Knapp, M., Manthorpe, J., Moran, N., Netten, A., Stevens, M. and Wilberforce, M. (2008) *Evaluation of the Individual Budgets Pilot Programme: Final Report*, York: Social Policy Research Unit, University of York

Glynn, M., Beresford, P. with Bewley, C., Branfield, F., Butt, J., Croft, S., Dattani Pitt, K., Fleming, J., Flynn, J., Patmore, C., Postle, K. and Turner, M. (2008) *Person Centred Support. What Service Users and Practitioners Say*, York: Joseph Rowntree Foundation

Glynos, J. (2001) 'The grip of ideology', *Journal of Political Ideologies*, Vol. 6, No. 2, pp. 191–214; doi: 10.1080/1356931012005385 8

Governance International (2011) *What You Always Wanted to Know About Co-production*. Available at URL: www.govint.org/english/main-menu/our-services/engagement/co-production-tree (accessed 4 August 2014)

Hall, E. (2011) 'Shopping for support: Personalisation and the new spaces and relations of commodified care for people with learning disabilities', *Social and Cultural Geography*, Vol. 12, p. 6; doi: 10.1080/14649365.2011.601236

Harris, J. and White, V. (eds.) (2009) *Modernising Social Work: Critical Considerations*, Bristol: Policy Press

Hartley, J. (2005). 'Innovation in governance and public services: Past and present', *Public Money and Management*, Vol. 25, No. 1, pp. 27–34; doi: 10.1111/j.1467–9302.2005.00447.x

Hatton, C. and Waters, J. (2013) *The Second (POET): Survey of Personal Budget Holders and Carers*, London: *In Control* Publications

Hauben, H., Coucheir, M., Spooren, J., McAnaney, D. and Delfosse, C. (2012) *Assessing the Impact of European Government's Austerity Plans on the Rights of People with Disabilities*. Available at URL: www.enil.eu/wp-content/uploads/2012/12/Austerity-European-Report_FINAL.pdf (accessed 22 May 2013)

Heise, A. and Lierse, H. (2011) 'Budget consolidation and the European social model the effects of European austerity programmes on social security systems', *Modern Economy*, Vol. 2, pp. 498–513; doi: 10.4236/me.2011.24055

HM Government (2007) *Putting People First: A Shared Vision and Commitment to the Transformation of Adult Social Care*. Available at URL: http://webarchive.nationalarchives.gov.uk/20130107105354/www.dh.gov.uk/prod_consum_dh/groups/dh_digitalassets/@dh/@en/documents/digitalasset/dh_081119.pdf (accessed 4 August 2014)

Homer, T. and Gilder, P. (2008), *A Review of Self-directed Support in Scotland*, Social Research Report, Edinburgh: Scottish Government

Hunter, S., Manthorpe, J., Ridley, J., Cornes, M. and Rosengard, A. (2012) 'When self-directed support meets adult support and protection: Findings from the evaluation of the SDS test sites in Scotland', *Journal of Adult Protection*, Vol. 4, pp. 205–15; doi: 10.1108/14668201211256717

Hunter, S. and Ritchie, P. (2007) *Co-production and Personalisation in Social Care: Changing Relationships in the Provision of Social Care*, Research Highlights No. 49, London: Jessica Kingsley

Hunter, S. and Rowley, D. (under review) *Better Services, Better Lives*, Bristol: Policy Press

IRISS (2014) *Pilotlight: Using Evidence to Light the Pathway for Providers of SDS*. Available at URL: http://pilotlight.iriss.org.uk (accessed 14 April 2014)

Jacobs, S., Abell, J., Stevens, M., Wilberforce, M., Challis, D., Manthorpe, J., Fernandez, J. L., Glendinning, C., Jones, K., Knapp, M., Moran, N., and Netten, A. (2013) 'The personalization of care services and the early impact on staff activity patterns', *Journal of Social Work*, Vol. 13, No. 2, pp. 141–63; doi: 10.1177/1468017311410681

Johnston, L. and Quarriers in association with Lardner, C., Barton, A. and Martin, M. (2009) *The Capacity of Disability Organisations to Engage with Public Authorities*, Edinburgh: Scottish Government Social Research

Joseph Rowntree Foundation (2011) *Sustaining Social Care: Transforming Social Support*, York, Joseph Rowntree Foundation. Available at URL: www.jrf.org. uk/sites/files/jrf/social-care-personal-support-summary.pdf (accessed 27 March 2014)

Karanikolas, M., Mladovsky, P., Thomson, S., Basu, S., Stuckler, D., Mackenbach, J. and McKee, M. (2013) 'Financial crisis, austerity, and health in Europe', *The Lancet*, Vol. 381, pp. 1323–31

Kestenbaum, A. (1992) *Cash for Care: The Experience of Independent Living Clients*, Nottingham: Independent Living Fund

Kettle, M., O'Donnell, J. and Newman, S. (2011) 'Getting together and being personal: Building personalization on a co-production approach', *Journal of Care Services Management*, Vol. 5, No. 1, pp. 29–34; doi: 10.1179/17501681 1X12883685966891

Kinder, T. (2012) 'Learning, innovating and performance in post-new public management of locally delivered public services', *Public Management Review*, Vol. 14, No. 3, pp. 403–28

Lapsley, I. (2009) 'New public management: The cruellest invention of the human spirit?', *ABACUS*, Vol. 45, No. 1, pp. 1–21; doi: 10.1111/j.1467–6281.2009.00275.x

Leadbeater, C. (2004) *Personalisation Through Participation: A New Script for Public Services*, London: Demos

Leadbeater, C. (2008) *We Think: Mass Innovation Not Mass Production*, London: Profile Books

Leadbeater, C. and Lownsbrough, H. (2005) *Personalisation and Participation: The Future of Social Care in Scotland*, London: Demos

Leece, J. and Leece, D. (2011) 'Personalisation: Perceptions of the role of social work in a world of brokers and budgets', *British Journal of Social Work*, Vol. 41, pp. 204–23; doi: 10.1093/bjsw/bcq087

Loeffler, E., Parrado, S., Bovaird, T. and van Ryzin, G. (2008) *'If You Want to Go Fast, Walk Alone. If You Want to Go Far, Walk Together': Citizens and the Co-production of Public Services, Report to the EU Presidency*, Paris, Ministry of Finance, Budget and Public Services

London SDS Forum (2013) *Making Personalisation Work in London*, London: SDS Forum

Lymbery, M. (2012) 'Social work and personalisation', *British Journal of Social Work*, November; doi: 101093/bjsw/bcs165

Lymbery, M. and Morley, K. (2012) 'Self-directed support and social work practice', *Social Work in Action*, Vol. 24, No. 5, pp. 315–27; doi: 10.1080/09503153.2012.743983

Main, J. (2013) 'Personalisation – *Plus ca change?*', in Beresford, P. (ed.) (2013) *Personalisation*, Bristol: Policy Press; available as e-book

Manthorpe, J., Hindes, J., Martineau, S., Cornes, M., Ridley, J., Spandler, H., Rosengard, A., Hunter, S., Little, S. and Gray, B. (2011) *Self-directed Support: A Review of the Barriers and Facilitators*. Available at URL: www.scotland.gov. uk/Publications/2011/03/30091835/0 (accessed 29 January 2014)

Manthorpe, J., Martineau, S., Ridley, J., Cornes, M., Rosengard, A. and Hunter, S. (2014) 'Embarking on self-directed support in Scotland: A focused scoping review of the literature', *European Journal of Social Work*; doi: 10.1080/13691457.2014.885883

Manthorpe, J., Stevens, M., Rapaport, J., Jacobs, S., Challis, D., Wilberforce, M., Netten, A., Knapp, M. and Glendinning, C. (2010a) 'Gearing up for personalisation: Training activities commissioned in the English pilot individual budget sites 2006–2008', *Social Work Education*, Vol. 29, No. 3, pp. 319–31; doi: 10.1080/02615470902913175

Manthorpe, J., Stevens, M., Rapaport, J., Challis, D., Jacobs, S., Netten, A., Jones, K., Knapp, M., Wilberforce, M. and Glendinning, C. (2010b) 'Individual budgets and adult safeguarding: Parallel or converging tracks. Further findings from the evaluation of the individual budget pilots', *Journal of Social Work*, 21 September; doi: 10.1177/1468017310379452

Miller, E. (2012), *Individual Outcomes: Getting Back to What Matters*, Dunedin Academic Press, Edinburgh

Mind (2009) *Personalisation in Mental Health: Breaking Down the Barriers. a Guide for Care Coordinators*, London: Mind

Morris, J. (2004) 'Independent living and community care: A disempowering framework', *Disability & Society*, Vol. 19, No. 5, pp. 427–42; doi: 10.1080/0968759042000235280

Morris, J. (2014) *Personal Budgets and Self-determination*. Available at URL: http://jennymorrisnet.blogspot.co.uk/2014/04/personal-budgets-and-self-determination.html (accessed 29 May 2014)

Needham, C. (2011a) 'Personalization: From story-line to practice', *Social Policy and Administration*, Vol. 45, No. 1, pp. 54–68; doi: 10.1111/j.1467–9515.2010.00753.x

Needham, C. (2011b) *Personalising Public Services. Understanding the Personalization Narrative*, Bristol: Policy Press

Needham, C. (2013) 'Personalisation: From day centres to community hubs?', *Critical Social Policy*, Vol. 34, No. 1, pp. 90–108; doi: 10.1177/0261018313481564

Needham, C. and Carr, S. (2009) *Co-production: an emerging evidence base for adult care transformation*. Research Briefing No. 31, London: Social Care Institute for Excellence

Nesta (2011) *Co-production Phase 2: Taking Co-production to Scale in Services for Patients with Long Term Health Conditions, Strategic Partners – Call for Proposals*, London: Nesta

Newbronner, L., Chamberlain, R., Bosanquet, K., Bartlett, C., Sass, B. and Glendinning, C. (2011) *Keeping Personal Budgets Personal: Learning from the Experiences of Older People with Mental Health Problems and Their Carers*, Research Briefing No. 40, London: Social Care Institute for Excellence

Oliver, M. and Barnes, C. (1998) *Disabled People and Social Policy: From Exclusion to Inclusion*, London: Longman

Osborne, S. P. (2006) 'The new public governance', *Public Management Review*, Vol. 8, No. 3, pp. 377–87; doi: 10.1080/14719030600853022

Osborne, S. P. (ed.) (2009) *The New Public Governance? Emerging Perspectives on the Theory and Practice of Public Governance*, London: Routledge

Ottmann, G., Laragy, C., Allen, J. and Feldman, P. (2011) 'Participatory action research to develop a model of community aged care', *Systematic Practice Action Research*, Vol. 24, pp. 413–27

Owen, P. (2013) 'Every coalition U-turn: The list in full', *The Guardian*, 7 February. Available at URL: www.theguardian.com/politics/2012/may/31/coalition-u-turns-full-list (accessed 5 March)

Parker, S. (2014) 'NHS Better Care Fund postponed – what is really going on?', http://www.theguardian.com/local-government-network/2014/may/07/nhs-better-care-fund-policy-delayed (accessed September 2014)

Pearson, C. (2000) 'Money talks? Competing discourses in the implementation of direct payments', *Critical Social Policy*, Vol. 20, pp. 459–77; doi: 10.1177/026101830002000403

Pearson, C. (2004) 'Keeping the cash under control: What's the problem with direct payments in Scotland?', *Disability & Society*, Vol. 19, No. 1. pp. 3–14; doi: 10.1080/0968759032000155596

Pearson, C. (ed.) (2006) *Direct Payments and the Personalisation of Care*, Edinburgh: Dunedin Academic Press

Pestoff, V. (2012) 'Co-production and the third sector social services in Europe: Some concepts and evidence', *Voluntas*, Vol. 23, pp. 1102–18; doi: 10.1007/s11266–012–9308–7

Pile, H. (2013) 'All in the name of personalization', in Beresford, P. (ed.) *Personalisation*, Bristol: Policy Press; available as e-book

Poll, C., Duffy, S., Hatton, C., Sanderson, H. and Routledge, M. (2006) *A Report on In Control's First Phase 2003–2005*. Available from URL: www.in-control.org.uk/media/55724/in%20control%20first%20phase%20report%202003–2005.pdf (accessed 28 January 2014)

Power, A., Lord, J. E. and DeFranco, A. S. (2013) *Active Citizenship and Disability: Implementing the Personalisation of Support*, Cambridge: Cambridge University Press

Powell, J. (2012) Personalisation and community care: A case study of the British system', *Ageing International*, Vol. 37, pp. 16–24; doi: 10.1007/s12126–011–9139–7

Priestley, M., Riddell, S., Jolly, D., Pearson, C., Williams, V., Barnes, C. and Mercer, G. (2010) 'Cultures of welfare at the front line: Implementing direct payments for disabled people in the UK', *Policy & Politics*, Vol. 38, No. 2, p. 307; doi: 10.1332/030557309X477956

Providers & Personalisation (2014) *Self-directed Support, Regulation and Inspection Research*, Edinburgh: Providers & Personalisation/Coalition of Care and Support Providers

Rabiee, P. (2012) 'Exploring the relationship between choice and independence: Experiences of disabled and older people', *British Journal of Social Work*, Vol. 43, No. 5, pp. 872–88; doi: 10.1093/bjsw/bcs022

Rabiee, P., Moran, N. and Glendinning, C. (2009) 'Individual budgets: Lessons from early users' experiences', *British Journal of Social Work*, Vol. 39, pp. 918–35

Ratza, A. (2012) *Personal Assistance and the Crisis: Now is the Time to Promote Direct Payments for Personal Assistance*. Available from URL: www.independentliving.org/node/1195 (accessed 27 March 2014)

Reid Howie Associates (2010) *Study of the Workforce and Employment Issues Surrounding Self-directed Support*, Edinburgh: Scottish Government Social Research

Renshaw, C. (2008) 'Do self-assessment and self-directed support undermine traditional social work with disabled people?, *Disability & Society*, Vol. 23, No. 3, pp. 283–6; doi: 10.1080/09687590801954075

Riddell, S., Ahlgren, L., Pearson, C., Williams, V., Watson, N. and MacFarlane, H. (2006), *The Implementation of Direct Payments for People Who Use Care Services*, SP paper No. 624, Edinburgh: Health Committee Report to Scottish Parliament

Riddell, S., Pearson, C., Barnes, C., Jolly, D., Mercer, G. and Priestley, M. (2005) 'The development of direct payments in the UK: Implications for social justice', *Social Policy and Society*, Vol. 4, No. 1, pp. 75–85; doi: 10.1017/S1474746404002209

Ridley, J. (2006) 'Direct what?' Exploring the suitability of direct payments for people with mental health problems', in Leece, J. and Bornat, J. (eds) (2006) *Developments in Direct Payments*, Bristol: Policy Press

Ridley, J., Spandler, H., Rosengard, A., Little, S., Cornes, M., Manthorpe, J., Hunter, S., Kinder, T. and Gray, B. (2011), *Evaluation of Self-directed Support Test Sites in Scotland*, Edinburgh: Scottish Government Social Research

Ridley, J., Spandler, H., Rosengard, A. with Menhennet, A. (2012) *Follow-up Evaluation of Self-directed Support Test Sites in Scotland*, Edinburgh: Scottish Government Social Research

Roll, J. (1996) *The Community Care (Direct Payments) Bill: Research Paper*, London: House of Commons Library

Rosengard, A., Ridley, J. and Manthorpe, J. (2013) 'Housing support and personalisation: Observations from the Scottish self-directed support test sites', *Housing, Care and Support*, Vol. 16, No. 3, pp. 1–9; doi: 10.1108/HCS-08-2013-0011

Roulstone, A., Harrington, B. and Se Kwang Hang, (2013) 'Flexible and personalised? An evaluation of a UK tailored employment support programme for jobseekers with enduring mental health problems and learning difficulties', *Scandinavian Journal of Disability Research*; doi: 10.1080/15017419.2012.761157

Roulstone, A. and Morgan, H. (2009) 'Neo-liberal individualism or self-directed support: Are we all speaking the same language on modernising adult social care?', *Social Policy and Society*, Vol. 8, No. 3, pp. 333–45; doi: 10.1017/S1474746409004886

Rummery, K. (2006) 'Disabled citizens and social exclusion: The role of direct payments', *Policy & Politics*, Vol. 34, No. 4, pp. 633–51; doi: 10.1177/0261018309105177

Rummery, K., Bell, D., Bowes, A., Dawson, A. and Roberts, E. (2012) *Counting the Costs of Choice and Control: Evidence for the Costs of Self-directed Support in Scotland*. Available from URL: www.scotland.gov.uk/Publications/2012/02/9547/0 (accessed 24 September 2012)

Samuel, M. (2012) '600,000 disabled people to lose out on benefits by 2018', *Community Care*. Available from URL: www.

communitycare.co.uk/2012/12/14/600000-disabled-people-to-lose-out-on-benefits-by-2018/#.Us5wemRdUig (accessed 9 January 2013)

Scottish Executive (2006) *Changing Lives: Report of the 21st Century Social Work Review in Scotland*, Edinburgh: Scottish Executive. Available from URL: http://www.scotland.gov.uk/Publications/2006/02/02094408/0 (accessed 4 August 2014)

Scottish Government (2007) *Better Health, Better Care: Action Plan*. Available from URL: www.scotland.gov.uk/Resource/Doc/206458/0054871.pdf (accessed 3 April 2014)

Scottish Government (2010) *Self-directed Support: A National Strategy for Scotland*. Available from URL: www.scotland.gov.uk/Publications/2010/02/05133942/0 (accessed 27 February 2014)

Scottish Government (2012) *Scotland's Spending Plans and Draft Budget 2012–13*. Available from URL: www.scotland.gov.uk/Topics/Government/Finance/18127 (accessed 31 March 2014)

Scottish Government (2013) *Social Care (Self-directed Support) (Scotland) Act*. Available at URL: www.legislation.gov.uk/asp/2013/1/contents (accessed 4 August 2014)

Scottish Government (2014a) *UK Government Cuts to Welfare Spending in Scotland – Budget 2014*. Available from URL: www.scotland.gov.uk/Topics/People/welfarereform/analysis/ukgwelfarecutsbudg2014 (accessed 10 April 2014)

Scottish Government (2014b) *Scottish Independent Living Fund*. Available from URL: http://news.scotland.gov.uk/News/Scottish-Independent-Living-Fund-b69.aspx (accessed 14 April 2014)

Scottish Government (2014c) *Statutory Guidance to Accompany the Social Care (Self-directed Support) (Scotland) Act 2013*, Edinburgh: Scottish Government

Scourfield, P. (2005) 'Implementing the Community Care (Direct Payments) Act: Will the supply of personal assistants meet the demand and at what price?', *Journal of Social Policy*, Vol. 34, No. 3, pp. 1–20

Self-directed Support Scotland (2013) *Self-directed Support: Implementation of the SDS Strategy and Bill. 'Stock Take' Questionnaire. Analysis Report*. Available at www.selfdirectedsupportscotland.org.uk/strategy/local-authority-implementation (accessed on 13 March 2014)

Series, L. and Clements, L. (2013) 'Putting the cart before the horse: Resource allocation systems and community care', *Journal of Social Welfare and Family Law*, Vol. 35, No. 2, pp. 207–26; doi: 10.1080/09649069.2013.800288

Slasberg, C., Beresford, P. and Schofield, P. (2012) 'Can personal budgets really deliver better outcomes for all at no cost?', *Disability & Society*, Vol. 27, No. 7, pp. 1029–34; doi: 10.1080/09687599.2012.736671

Slasberg, C., Beresford, P. and Schofield, P. (2013) 'The increasing evidence of how SDS is failing to deliver personal budgets and personalisation', *Research, Policy and Planning*, Vol. 30, No. 2, pp. 91–105; doi: 10.1080/69687599.2012.695576

Smith, M., Wilkinson, H. and Gallagher, M. (2013) ' "It's what gets through people's radars isn't it": Relationships in social work practice and knowledge exchange', *Contemporary Social Science*, Vol. 9, No. 3, pp. 292–306; doi: 10.1080/21582041.2012.751499

Stack, P. (2013) 'The need for true person-centred support', in Beresford, P. (ed.) (2013) *Personalisation*, Bristol: Policy Press; available as e-book

Taylor, M., Hoyes, L., Lart, R. and Means, R. (1992) *User Empowerment in Community Care: Unravelling the Issues*, DQM Paper No. 11, Bristol: School for Advanced Urban Studies

Trevisan, F. (2013) 'Disabled people, digital campaigns, and contentious politics: Upload successful or connection failed?,' in Scullion, R., Lilleker, D., Jackson, D. and Gerodimos, R. (eds), *The Media, Political Participation, and Empowerment*, London: Routledge, pp. 175–91

Vallelly, S. and Manthorpe J. (2009) 'Choice and control in specialist housing: Starting conversations between commissioners and providers', *Housing Care and Support*, Vol. 12, No. 2, pp. 9–15; doi: 10.1108/14608790200900009

Vamstad, J. (2004) 'Co-production as a defining principle – a new typology for provision of welfare services in Sweden', paper given at European Group for Public Administration conference, Ljubljana, Slovenia

Verschuere, B., Brandsen, T. and Pestoff, V. (2012) 'Co-production: The state of art in research and the future agenda', *Voluntas*, Vol. 23, pp. 1083–101

Watt, N. (2014) 'Holyrood given power to end "bedroom tax" in Scotland', *The Guardian*, 2 May. Available at URL: www.theguardian.com/society/2014/may/02/holyrood-power-end-bedroom-tax-scotland (accessed 28 May 2014)

West, K. (2013) 'The grip of personalization in adult social care: Between managerial domination and fantasy', *Critical Social Policy*, Vol. 33, No. 4, pp. 638–57; doi: 10.1177/0261018313481563

White, A. (2013) 'The secret cuts part two: The ILF', *New Statesman*, 6 June. Available at URL: www.newstatesman.com/politics/2013/06/secret-cuts-part-two-independent-living-fund (accessed 29 August 2013)

Willsher, K. (2012) 'France turns corner on disability – but austerity threatens further progress', *The Guardian*, 28 September. Available at URL: www.theguardian.com/world/2012/sep/28/france-disability-progress-austerity (accessed 28 January 2014)

Witcher, S. (2013) *Inclusive Equality: A Vision for Social Justice*, Bristol: Policy Press

Witcher, S. (2014) *My Choices: A Vision for Self-directed Support*, Glasgow: Glasgow Disability Alliance

Witcher, S., Stalker, K., Roadburg, M. and Jones, C. (2000), *Direct Payments: The Impact on Choice and Control for Disabled People*, Edinburgh: Scottish Executive Central Research Unit

Wood, C. (2011) *Personal Best*. Available from URL: www.demos.co.uk/publications/personalbest (accessed 3 April 2014)

Wood, C., Cheetham, P. and Gregory, T. (2012) *Coping with the Cuts*, Available from URL: www.demos.co.uk/publications/copingwiththecuts (accessed 31 March 2014)

Wood, C. and Grant, E. (2010) *For Disabled People, Cuts to Welfare Will Have a Deep and Lasting Impact: Destination Unknown*. Available from URL: www.demos.co.uk/publications/destinationunknowndisability (accessed 31 March 2014)

Wood, C. and Grant, E. (2012): *Destination Unknown: For Disabled People the*

Worst Is Yet to Come. Available from URL: www.demos.co.uk/publications/ destinationunknownsummer2012 (accessed 31 March 2014)

Young, A. (2010) 'Commentary. Personalisation: Can social workers face it? A personal experience', *Journal of Social Work Practice,* Vol. 24, No. 3, pp. 315–17; doi: 10.1080/02650533.2010.500128

Zarb, G. (2013) *Personalisation Now Independent Living Lite.* Available from URL: http://disabilityrightsuk.org/news/2013/november/personalisation-now-independent living-lite (accessed 12 November 2013)

Zarb, G. and Nadash, P. (1994) *Cashing in on Independence: Comparing the Cost and Benefits of Cash and Services,* Somercotes, Derbyshire: British Council of Organisations of Disabled People

FURTHER READING

ADASS (2009) *Personalisation and the Law: Implementing Putting People First in the Current Legal Framework*, London: Association of Directors of Adult Social Services

Arnstein, S. (1974) 'The ladder of citizen participation', *Journal of the Royal Town Planning Institute*, Vol. 57, pp. 176–82

Carey, M. (2009) 'Critical commentary: Happy shopper? The problem with service user and carer participation', *British Journal of Social Work*, Vol. 39, No. 1, pp. 179–88; doi: 10.1093/bjsw/bcn166

Cross, M. (2013) 'Demonised, impoverished and now forced into isolation: The fate of disabled people under austerity', *Disability & Society*, Vol. 28, No. 5, pp. 719–23; doi: 10.1080/09687599.2013.808087

Cutler, T., Waine, B. and Brehony, K. (2007) 'A new epoch of individualization? Problems with the personalization of public services', *Public Administration*, Vol. 85, No. 3, pp. 847–55; doi: 10.1111/j.1467–9299.2007.00672.x

Department of Health (2012) *Transforming Care: A National Response to Winterbourne Hospital. Final Report*, London: Department of Health. Available at URL: https://www.gov.uk/government/uploads/system/uploads/attachment_data/file/213215/final-report.pdf (accessed 4 December 2013)

Department for Work and Pensions (2012) *Personal Independence Payments: Assessment Thresholds*, London: Department for Work and Pensions

Houston, S. (2010) 'Beyond *Homo economicus*: Recognition, self-realization and social work', *British Journal of Social Work*, Vol. 40, pp. 841–57; doi: 10.1093/bjsw/bcn132

Huxham, C. and Vangen, S. (2005) *Managing to Collaborate. The Theory and Practice of Collaborative Advantage*, London: Routledge

Kinder, T., Radnor, Z. and Osborne, S., 'User-led innovation and co-production in the service-dominant approach to public services' (unpublished paper)

Malik, S. (2013) 'Bedroom tax legal challenge dismissed by high court', *The Guardian*, 30 July. Available at URL: www.theguardian.com/society/2013/jul/30/bedroom-tax-legal-high-court (accessed 4 August 2014)

Priestley, M., Jolly, D., Pearson, C., Riddell, S., Barnes, C. and Mercer, G. (2007) 'Direct payments and disabled people in the UK: Supply, demand and devolution', *British Journal of Social Work*, Vol. 37, pp. 1189–204; doi: 10.1093/bjsw/bc1063

Rabiee, P. and Glendinning, C. (2010) 'Choice: What, when and why? Exploring the importance of choice to disabled people', *Disability & Society*, Vol. 25, No. 7, pp. 827–40

Scottish Executive (2000) *Adults with Incapacity (Scotland) Act*. Available at URL: www.scotland.gov.uk/Topics/Justice/law/awi (accessed 4 August 2014)

Scottish Executive (2003) *Mental Health (Care and Treatment) (Scotland) Act*. Available at URL: www.legislation.gov.uk/asp/2003/13/contents (accessed 4 August 2014)

Socialstyrelsen (2009) *Swedish Disability Policy – Service and Care for People with Functional Impairments*, Stockholm: Socialstyrelsen. Available from URL: www.socialstyrelsen.se/lists/Artikelkatalog/Attach-ments/8407/2009-126-188_2009126188.pdf (accessed 21 August 2014)

Spiker, P. (2012) 'Personalisation falls short', *British Journal of Social Work*, pp. 1–17; doi:10.1093/bjsw/bcs063

INDEX

Note: page numbers in *italics* denote tables or figures